11⁵⁰

Town Planning in its Social Context

Town Planning in its Social Context

Gordon E. Cherry

BA, MTPI, FRICS

LEONARD HILL
LONDON: 1970

Published by
Leonard Hill Books.
A division of
International Textbook Company Ltd
158 Buckingham Palace Road, London, SW1
© 1970 G. E. Cherry
First published 1970
ISBN 0 249 44026 1

Printed in Great Britain by
Butler & Tanner Ltd, Frome and London

TO SHONA AND SHELAGH

'The politics of the future are
social politics and the problem is
still how to secure the greatest
happiness of the greatest number,
and especially of those whom all
previous legislation and reform
seem to have left very much
where they were before.' (Joseph
Chamberlain)

Contents

Introduction

1 The Social Tradition in Town Planning   9

2 Social Objectives of Town Planning   42

3 Social Issues for the Town Planner   57

4 A Framework for Social Planning Policies   115

5 Summary, Conclusions and Implications   163

Index   179

Acknowledgements

My acknowledgements are due to a large number of people. At the outset I should mention Dr Wilfred Burns, Chief Planner, Ministry of Housing and Local Government, formerly City Planning Officer, Newcastle upon Tyne, who first suggested the idea of this book to me. The opportunity of working in his Department, where the accumulated experience of professional colleagues was so valuable, made for a stimulating working environment. The concept of social planning which I have developed owes much to those formative years of contact with people too numerous to mention, but if they read this book they will recognize the depth of their contribution.

I should speak in similar vein of valued contact with colleagues at the Centre for Urban and Regional Studies. I am grateful for this exposure to new experiences and outlooks.

My thanks are due in particular to those who read this book in draft and were kind enough to offer valuable criticisms and advice: Professor E. A. Rose, Mr and Mrs G. Brooke Taylor, and Professor J. B. Cullingworth to whom especially I am indebted.

To all these people I must of course say that the inevitable limitations of this book are entirely mine.

I am grateful for permission to reproduce illustrations kindly supplied by Mr J. Bebbington, City Librarian, Sheffield (Plates I and II); the *Birmingham Post* (Plates V and X); Mr R. J. A. Gazzard, Director of Development, Killingworth (Plate VI); Mr B. Warren, City Architect, Sheffield (Plate VII); Mr K. A. Galley, City Planning Officer, Newcastle upon Tyne (Plates VIII and IX); and to Messrs Faber & Faber for permission to reproduce from *Garden Cities of Tomorrow* (Plates III and IV).

I should thank sincerely my secretary Mrs Jacky Bulgin for her patience and skill in helping me with this work.

Literary work is a lonely occupation. Finally I must express the continual sense of gratitude to my wife, Margaret, for sharing the isolation.

GORDON E. CHERRY

Centre for Urban and Regional Studies
University of Birmingham
March 1970

Introduction

Various meanings may be ascribed to the term 'social planning'. To some people it may suggest social engineering in an idealistic sense following some utopian concept. To others it may have a more particular base, for example the organization of resources to combat poverty or racial discrimination. Alternatively, on a broader front again, it might be seen as the co-ordination of social work undertaken by various agencies over a given geographical area. From a governmental point of view it might refer at either local, regional or national level to the co-ordination of health and welfare services and policy making in this field. To others the term 'social development planning' may be more precise when what is implied is the planning of social services with regard to particular communities, especially new communities.

The term may therefore cover different interpretations, and it is clearly wise at the outset to begin definitively. The idea of social planning has been taken up increasingly by the town planner in recent years, and it is his concepts which are examined here. This book outlines the social context of town planning: in relation to this theme I suggest that the particular field of social planning might be defined as a contributory specialism within town planning itself, dependent on the parent subject but with its own coherent range of interest and study.

This review of the principles and practice of social planning allows for a timely examination of the spirit and purpose of town planning as a whole. On occasions in the past it has been fashionable for planners to have pronounced views about social objectives, but the present time is not one of them. While there seems to be general confusion about the broad goals of planning and how they might be achieved, there are mistrust and doubts particularly about social objectives. Many of these have been inherited from the very early days of the planning movement, and although they are clearly difficult to interpret in a modern context without real understanding of the historical setting within which they were formulated, nevertheless a re-evaluation of basic principles indicates that the social philosophy of planning might now be expressed afresh within the comprehensive scope of physical, social and economic planning. This book suggests an approach and reviews the implications.

Successively during the twentieth century, town planning has been concerned with an ever-increasing range of questions: for example, the design and layout of residential areas, and later, town centres, industrial areas and other elements of the planned environment; the allocation of land use and the co-ordination of development; national economic problems such as the distribution of industry and employment; regional matters; recreation; and traffic and transportation. For administrative and technical reasons this has tended to result in a compartmented structure of the planning process and incidentally to erode a central philosophy. Quite apart from the competing claims of other disciplines, within town planning itself there has tended to be fragmentation, with each contributory field seeking its own identity rather than acknowledging an interlocking relationship.

This must not be overstated, but it is true to say that the practising town planner finds it easy to lose sight of the meaning of the end product of his work in the context of total planning objectives. The person both carrying out day-to-day administrative tasks and engaged in detailed technical considerations of a particular project may be blind to the relevance of his work to any central theme; in any case the time scale is such in planning that there are difficulties in relating goal setting to attainment within a manageable period. This is not to say however that the practising planner is denied satisfaction by reason of an inability to grasp the purpose of his work. He may for example find satisfaction in the machinery of planning for reasons such as the exercise of power (real or otherwise) or a bureaucratic predilection for the decision-taking process and the achievement of order. But the planning profession as a whole, as well as individuals both within the professional body and outside it, is searching for a reappraisal of the spirit and purpose of planning's area of concern.

The standpoint described here emphasizes the social base of town planning. It attempts to rediscover this core, and suggests how this leads the planner into participating in a new and wide field of social questions. In essence there is nothing new in the fundamental argument which recognizes social objectives; but the restatement involves a new interpretation, and it is this which necessitates a new outlook.

Chapter 1 reviews the utopian tradition in the social solutions which have been posed in the past, and identifies the various strands, particularly of the nineteenth century, which have gone to make up the composition of the town planning movement. Chapter 2 looks at social objectives of town planning at the present time. Chapter 3 examines some of the contemporary social issues for the town planner, and Chapter 4 looks at a possible framework for social planning policies. Chapter 5 draws together the main conclusions and offers a number of implications for planners and their professional body.

This coverage cannot pretend to be detailed and comprehensive, but this is not the intention. This book in no way sets out to be a textbook on social planning, affording an outline of practice. It is, rather, an approach, and a consciously selective one at that, heavily dependent on personal experience and narrowed by an incomplete awareness of the full range of relevant material on which to draw. The book does however seek to make a contribution to town planning by reinterpreting its central philosophy and outlining some of the pertinent issues in a newly recognized field of concern.

The ideas for this book crystallized during my time as Research Officer in the City Planning Department, Newcastle upon Tyne. The Department under the dynamic leadership of Dr Wilfred Burns both recognized and developed the social content of planning, and in the period 1964–8 I was privileged to be associated with planning work of a very advanced kind. The *City Development Plan* of 1963, a review of the first submission, set the scene by including the following statement: 'There is a growing volume of sociological research work on neighbourhoods and housing estates and it is now becoming important to follow this through into new social policies to give the optimum conditions for the varied groups living within the City. This "Social Plan" will be formulated within the early years of the Plan period.' The preparation of the Social Plan was in fact approached through work on a variety of matters concerned with situations in the city, and this experience of being involved in a developing exercise concerning both research and implementation of policy was not only extremely valuable but also well-nigh unique in a local authority planning department in this country at that time.

The work was first developed in connection with housing. The Report *Housing—a Review of Current Problems and Policies* (1964) supplemented an earlier document *Towards a New Housing Policy—the Planning Base* (1962), and in two volumes brought together a number of related issues concerned with the supply of houses (both in terms of number and size of dwelling) and their improvement in the context of social and environmental factors.

Each year social surveys were conducted in respect of an area adjoining Scotswood Road in Newcastle. The character of the area was recorded in the early 1960s when slum clearance began, after which households were traced annually to their new accommodation either elsewhere in the city or back in the redevelopment area; this was to monitor changes in life styles and behaviour patterns and the housing satisfaction of those rehoused. The survey was therefore a long-term project designed to trace the social consequences of rehousing. For a number of reasons the study was not entirely successful, but useful insights were provided and experience gained in the carrying out of surveys of this type.

A constant theme during these years was the improvement of houses, and a particular contribution made at this time, as with a number of other progressive local authorities in the country, was an approach to the 'revitalization' of dwelling stock. This pioneer work added to the national debate about the improvement of older houses and subsequently there has been important new legislation in the Housing Act, 1969. The sociological aspects of this planning exercise were highlighted in the Rye Hill area proposals. The problems arose because the area selected for the improvement of living conditions became increasingly a social problem area, typical as a 'sump' concentration in the twilight area of most major cities. The process of confrontation of the planning machine with problems of poverty, deviants, immigrants, multi-occupation, problem families and the evidence of a transitional community in an area of urban decay was quite fascinating, and gave valuable experience for the development of a body of social planning theory and related expertise. The setting up of an Advisory Committee of the City Council with the Rye Hill Residents Association provided first-hand experience of a community participation process whereby representatives of a deprived neighbourhood faced a bureaucratic machine.

The Planning Department was also involved informally on personal levels with the promotion of sociological research, and there was ultimately a most valuable feedback. Two officers of the City Council, the City Planning Officer and the Medical Officer of Health, and two members, the former leader of the Council, Councillor T. Dan Smith and Councillor B. W. Abrahart, in addition to the Bishop of Newcastle, held early discussions as a result of which a university research project was set up, financed by a local Trust. The terms of reference, *inter alia*, were to investigate the obstacles in the way of normal families participating fully in community life, and to ascertain what resources and facilities were needed to provide the conditions for maximum human happiness. Professor P. Collison of the Department of Social Studies at Newcastle University took direction of the project in September 1965 and translated the objectives into research terms, selecting Rye Hill as an area of study. A Senior Research Associate, J. G. Davies, lived for a time in Rye Hill and engaged in 'participant observation'. His valuable findings were reported back to a steering committee of which I became secretary, and ultimately percolated through and contributed tremendously to an understanding of the characteristics of the area.

At the same time a major piece of social planning work in the Department was concerned with what became known in shorthand terms as 'social malaise'. With the co-operation of a number of officers of the Corporation and outside bodies, data were collected as to the distribution in the city of various aspects of physical ill-health (for example deaths from various causes or notification of disease), social ill-health (crime and delinquency statistics for instance) and mental ill-health. The mapping of these data revealed a very marked pattern of distribution, with a major concentration in a district immediately west of the central area, centred on Rye Hill. This spatial distribution was correlated with census evidence at Enumeration District level of various physical and socio-economic criteria. Selected aspects of the environment were found to be in a striking, positive correlation with the incidence of social malaise, and while there was no claim that this was a causal relationship, the need to harmonize physical and social planning activity was emphasized.

This work in turn stimulated an exercise concerning problem

families in the city. A Working Party of officers and members under the chairmanship of Councillor Mrs C. M. Lewcock, drew together the facts of the situation: a total of between 450 and 500 problem families, many of whom were concentrated in particular locations, were found to constitute a severe administrative problem, especially for the Director of Housing and the Medical Officer. The Planning Department's role was a full one, contributing to both survey and policy making in the Working Party's Report of 1966. The full planning involvement continued with subsequent negotiations over the setting up of a Family Service Unit in the city and administrative tasks in the Medical Officer's monitoring of problem families and their distribution.

Investigations into sections of the community continued with a major investigation into the condition of the immigrant groups in the city. This task fell readily into Planning Department activities and the research team was strengthened by the short-term appointment of an Indian sociologist, Sudha D. Telang. A policy document for the coloured immigrant in the city followed in 1967 covering all aspects of the Council's work. Again, the planning role did not stop at survey or even policy making on a broad front, but continued into subsequent administration and implementation: working with the Immigrants Liaison Committee, contact with immigrant groups towards the setting up of an Immigrants' Community Centre, and such work as the publication of a Hindi booklet welcoming newcomers to the city.

The involvement of the Department with social problems continued when in 1967 the Town Planning Committee set up a sub-committee of officers, members and outside representatives to look at the problem of prostitution with special reference to the Rye Hill area of the city.

An aspect of social planning concerns the contribution which might be made by the individual citizen in the planning process. The fact that the City Planning Officer was a member of the Planning Advisory Group set up by the Minister of Housing and Local Government to consider development plans was clearly relevant in the efforts made locally to stimulate citizen participation. The local plan for Jesmond, a vocal, largely middle class, but increasingly transitional area of Victorian Newcastle, provided the first experiment. The events of the first public meeting, held in a neighbourhood school, will long be remembered for the large numbers who turned up and for the type of meeting it turned out to be; equally from a professional point of view the experience of establishing a dialogue with residents' groups and associations over a long period was to be extremely valuable.

In quite a different field social planning became involved in leisure and recreation. Pilot work in 1966 into the leisure activities of a small sample of persons and schoolchildren in the city was carried out, followed by surveys into the use of swimming baths, children's playspaces and a Sports Centre. This was basic work towards the preparation of a plan for leisure for the city and was to be supplemented by major research exercises into the use of urban parks and attendances at city theatres. An Arts Working Group of the City Council was set up in 1967 of quite different composition from the previous Cultural Activities Committee, and the planning voice was heard on major policy objectives. Additionally, a major regional research exercise into outdoor recreation was launched in 1967, the findings of which will contribute to any possible reconsideration of provision of facilities in the city.

Another regional project in 1967 had been concerned with population migration. This contributed to a much greater understanding of a very dynamic element in the planning situation and an appreciation of the social forces which play their part in the process of population redistribution. As such, this fell well within the concern of social planning.

This catalogue of work does not pretend to be complete; it is merely to suggest how in one local planning authority at least the first strides have been made towards the recognition of a social planning element in the total town planning process. It indicates, too, how in practical terms the professional planner may interpret his wider terms of reference and actually get involved in issues far removed from what might have been regarded as traditional areas of work. It suggests what opportunities there are for interdepartmental working parties in an authority where Chief Officers are prepared to recognize that planning has this wider, all-embracing role. The cynic may still argue that all this was achieved because of the fortuitous coming together of personalities, important in both technical and political fields, but the fact remains that the examples of achievement has been presented. Out of that evidence the views and ideas contained in this book emerged.

Personal conclusions from the Newcastle work have been strengthened by exposure to a new set of circumstances outside local government and the world of the practising planner in the traditional sense. The Centre for Urban and Regional Studies in the University of Birmingham to which I now belong is a research institution (with a postgraduate teaching element) which focusses its work largely on the economic and social issues with which planning in its broad sense is concerned. The composition of the research staff is multi-disciplinary, and the research projects are making a very large planning contribution. This highlights the impossibility of defining precisely where town planning begins and ends; the edges are bound to be blurred, but at least as far as the social aspects are concerned my inclination is to set the boundaries much wider than attitudes have so far allowed.

1

The Social Tradition in
Town Planning

Utopian Heritage

Haverfield observed over half a century ago that town planning
was an act of intermittent activity, the conditions for which were
twofold.[1] In the first place, the period had to be one in which
towns were being founded or enlarged, and secondly, those
responsible for town building must care for the well-being of
common men and the proper arrangements of their dwellings.

It would not be claimed now that town planning was an intermittent activity, and the two main conditions for its development
might be expressed in rather a different way, but the once pertinent
observation is still helpful in identifying important features. We
can still stress that the development of the town planning movement during the twentieth century has rested on two main antecedents. One is a concern for urban form and the search for the
ideal city in architectural terms; the other is the search for the
ideal community. Frequently the two have gone hand in hand,
but they have different philosophical origins and methods of
expression, and both can be readily identified and examined.

Our main consideration here is the social aspect, and in the first
place we should recognize that forming part of, and constantly
subscribing to, the evolution of the British town planning movement, has been the underlying idealism of utopia. This, the
recurring dream of a perfect world, or a golden age, or simply of
a time and place where hard times were no more and injustices
were overcome, has been a repetitive product in history. Indeed,

Oscar Wilde's epigram that 'a map of the world that does not include Utopia is not even worth glancing at, for it leaves out the one country at which humanity is always landing' was a historical observation of some perception. Within this intellectual framework a variety of social experiments was conceived during the last century, out of which the town planning movement of the twentieth century has stemmed.

Utopian idealism has been expressed in different ways. One early form was the ethico-religious vision, such as that of the Old Testament prophets, continuing through with the teaching of Christ to St Augustine and St Thomas Aquinas. On the other hand the utopias of early Greece were essentially political in presentation. Both these roots were very apparent when utopian activity was resumed at the time of the Renaissance, and a series of literary utopias, beginning with that of Sir Thomas More, showed how new social systems might be conceived. In the nineteenth century utopian fervour was rekindled ('in this new world of falling water, burning coal and whirring machinery, utopia was born again,' as Mumford[2] puts it) and a large number of practical community experiments were made in the search for new social arrangements, social happiness or simply a much-needed improvement in the standard of urban life.

The tremendous variety of 'solutions' which have been put forward throughout history, either to counter specific problems or as ideals to follow in the pursuit of social progress, is well documented, and we can merely take a number of examples to illustrate the point. We might go back in time as far as the period 750–650 B.C. when four Old Testament prophets, Amos, Hosea, Isaiah and Micah, held their ministries. At this time Israel's prosperity was marked, but this was accompanied by corruption and social inequality. The four Hebrew prophets, together with Jeremiah and Ezekiel, emerged at this critical time, preaching lines of social reconstruction and depicting the perfect future; it may be claimed that Amos, the earliest, was a pioneer utopian. Together they worked to summon men back to a meaningful new life, proclaiming their conviction as to a social and religious purpose in life which was an answer to social and political problems in the national and international upheavals of the day.

This ethico-religious theme was fed, centuries later, by Christ and later still by the treatises of St Augustine (*de Civitate Dei*) and St Thomas Aquinas (*de Regimine Principum*). The strength of this underlying idealism was fanned into practical life from time to time, and as one example we might refer to an interesting social experiment at the close of the fifteenth century.

This was the attempt of Girolama Savonarola (1452–98) to establish a theocracy in Florence in 1494. Following the fall of the Medici in Florence strenuous efforts were made towards establishing a stable government. Savonarola, prior of San Marco, was stimulated to offer his theocratic vision of a strictly regulated Christian State, in which social and civic life was to be governed by Divine precepts, immorality was to be suppressed, private interests were to be subordinated to the common good and charity and equality were to be ubiquitous. Religious fervour, kindled with the spark of political excitement, fanned a rapid response to these ideals and for a short while in the exceptional climate of opinion Savonarola effected many remarkable reforms. But the experiment was doomed to failure. Inevitable reaction set in and the prior was ultimately burned at the stake.

But social 'solutions' in the past have also been put forward in political terms. The contribution of Plato, for example, came in Greece at the turn of the fourth century B.C. Student of Socrates, he produced his *Republic* in what was to become a very typical guise, postulating an ideal state as a myth rather than expressing his advanced ideas openly. He clearly inclined towards benevolent direction and accordingly his utopia was authoritarian and communistic. His solution was to divide society into three classes, each of which was to embody a particular virtue. The ruling class was to consist of philosophers, the second class being the guardians, including such as soldiers and public officials, while the third class was composed of the great mass of the people, workers and slaves. Given this hierarchy of rank, Plato considered that social regeneration could be effected through the organization of closely aggregated groups, each self-sufficient; his suggestion was that the groups should be represented by 5,040 heads of families.

In order to ensure that the individuals sublimated their own desires to the welfare of the state Plato severely restricted individualism by diminishing property and family rights. In the first place private property would be abolished and a system of communism established; in the second place child bearing and rearing would become a matter for the state, which could thereby exercise strong eugenic controls. Plato's utopian dream was in fact that man became a political animal, and this was to be ensured by securing his absorption into the state by wide comprehensive control, such as a system of education, censorship of the arts and by state super-vision of rank and occupation.

This socio-political solution continued with Aristotle, and with Plato these two philosophers were the first two 'western' thinkers to produce comprehensively organized analyses on a postulated form of social life. Phaleas, Xenophon and Phutarch continued the authoritarian trends of Hellenistic thought, but the genius that burst into flame in Ancient Greece was ultimately to be extinguished, and this branch of social idealism was truncated.

Concern about social problems and the regulation of society was brought to the fore again however with the Renaissance. The six-teenth and seventeenth centuries, a period of terrestrial explora-tions, scientific discoveries, social upheaval and philosophical fer-ment, witnessed the rebirth of utopian speculation. Indeed this period gave to the world not only the key word, but the book which gave its name to a whole class of literature, and the key personality, Thomas More. A study of his life and work is reward-with a population not to exceed 10,000, with eight main radial social experiment was nourished by his teaching.

Just as Plato wrote the *Republic* with the reformation of Athens as his concern, so More offered his literary treatise for the improve-ment of his country at a particularly difficult time. At home there was economic difficulty and poverty, a particular discontent being the dispossession of farm labourers from their homesteads so that arable land could be turned into pasture, and wool produced for the looms of Flanders. Politically, Europe was a chessboard of rivalries and aspirations for power by despots; and superimposed on these questions was the religious rethinking of the time and the intellectual break-through of the New Enlightenment.

The greater part of More's *Utopia* was written in Flanders. Written in the universal language, Latin, and published on the Continent in 1518, it was translated into German, Italian, French and Dutch within twenty years of his death; an English translation followed in 1551. The story is that of an imaginary narrator, Raphael Hythloday, and his wanderings, during which the country of Utopia is discovered and visited. Under this thin guise More gave his views on various social, political and religious questions of the day.

The constitution of the Utopians was supposed to date back to the conquest of the country by Utopus, 1,760 years before the time of Hythloday's visit. A confederation of free states each sent representatives to the general council of the central city,

Amaurote, the capital. The island contained, including Amaurote, 54 of these states, each consisting of a city with its shire, or adjacent territory. No two cities were less than 24 miles apart, nor more than a day's journey on foot. In each were 6,000 families, besides an indefinite number of persons living in farmsteads out in the shire. The households in these farmsteads consisted of 40 persons each, and the members came in rotation with the townspeople so that everyone had two years of country life in turn.

Each town family of Utopia was to have not fewer than ten nor more than sixteen children of the age of 14 or thereabouts allotted to it. Should the numbers in any one family become excessive, then the superabundance (overspill perhaps in modern terms!) was to be transferred to another that might be deficient. This principle was also followed where the population of a city became too large compared with another. If the population of the whole island became excessive then unoccupied land in adjacent countries was to be colonized.

From the point of view of government, every 30 families were under the authority of a Syphograunt, or a Phylarch; in turn every 10 Syphograunts came under a superior chief Phylarch, or a Tranibore. All were subject to annual election. The 200 Syphograunts elected a Prince, and the national island council met once a year. Municipal councils were held every third day or more often if required.

The principle of utopian life was community of goods. There was no private property, and there was no use of money except as a means of commercial intercourse with other nations. Accordingly, the organization of life was communistic; at regular intervals along each street there were halls in which the Syphograunts lived, and the 30 families attached to each went there for meals. Only about 500 persons in each city were excused from active labour, and life for the remainder was strictly regulated. There was to be six hours' work a day, three hours before dinner and three hours before supper. Lectures, music and games filled up intervals of the day; the day started at 4.00 a.m. and finished at 8.00 p.m.

This evidence of More's imagination has been given in some detail, for we should note that *Utopia* was no abstract programme. More's solution was a rigidly structured society, radically different from the one of his day. Moreover, the new society was conceived within the framework of a planned environment, in which the physical appearance of towns meant so much. In Amaurote for example we read that 'the stretes be appoynted and set forth verye commodious and handsome, bothe for carriage and also agaynst the wyndes. The houses be of fayre and gorgious buyldyng, and in the streete syde they stande ioyned together in a longe rowe throughe the hole streate without anye partition or separacion. The stretes be twenty fote brode. On the back syde of the houses, throughe the hole lengthe of the strete, lye large gardeynes, whyche be closed in rounde about with the backe parte of the stretes.' Later we are told that, 'they sett great stoore be theyre gardeins. In them they have vyneyardes, all manner of fruite, herbes, and flowres, so pleisaunte, so well furnished, and so fynelye kepte, that I never sawe thynge more fruitefull nor better trymmed in anny place.'[3]

Sir Thomas More developed, therefore, a carefully considered concept of man and society and he succeeded in drawing a particular picture of a corporate state. His influence was such that a succession of ideal postulates for society punctuated the sixteenth, seventeenth and eighteenth centuries. The best known are those of Tomaso Campanella, a Calabrian monk, with his book *City of the Sun*, of Johann Valentin Andreae, a German scholar, with his *Christianopolis* (1619), Francis Bacon's *New Atlantis* (1623), a scientific utopia, and James Harrington's *Oceana* (1656), a proposal for a new political constitution.

The ideal of utopia continued in subsequent years and was to feed its life blood into the stream of nineteenth-century thinking and activities. With both Hellenistic and Hebrew/Christian sources, the Renaissance produced its own particular version, and variations on this theme presented before every generation an ideal and goal for a society, which the medieval world could not accommodate.

From the Renaissance onwards the central characteristics of utopia rarely changed. For example, the ideal state was homocentric rather than theocentric; man had both the ability and obligation to change and improve his physical world and social systems. Economically, the utopias were based on centralization and control rather than freedom of individual activity. Socially, again the emphasis was on the group rather than the individual even to the extent that individual family life was curtailed; with education, in particular, the right of the state was raised above that of the parent, education being seen as a great agency for social solidarity. Utopias were not necessarily democratic; they seemed to operate best indeed as benevolent dictatorships. Plato conceived a tripartite division of society; More invented Syphograunts and Tranibores; and in Bacon's ideal state the laws established 2,000 years previously were so perfect that they need never be changed. And so it was that the cherished land was not frivolous; idealism was fervent and sincere and the lives offered were hard and earnest, but rewarding in the extreme. Finally, all utopias recognized the physical basis of social perfection, and the canon of environmental determinism supported all dreams of an ideal state; if the physical conditions of life are improved so will men's happiness be widened. This latter aspect in particular was an important feature of the social experiments of the nineteenth century and can be traced through into the evolving town planning movement of the twentieth century.

But the essence of Renaissance utopias was that they were myths; they were conceived and represented on far-away islands. More's Hythloday found the country of Utopus; Campanella's narrator recounts his visit to the state of Taprobane, situated on the equator; Andreae's *Christianopolis* was arranged on the island of Caphar Salama in the Antarctic; and Bacon's *New Atlantis* was found on an imaginary voyage from Peru when a ship was driven off course to the island of Bensalem.

This mythical representation might be thought to have weakened the utopian ideal. But successive settlements of persecuted sects in the New World derived much of their zeal from a utopian outlook. William Penn for example created his Philadelphia. Having extracted a land grant from Charles II in respect of Pennsylvania, he translated an ideal from myth to reality, laying out a town in 1681, establishing a government and undertaking a social experiment. He knew what sort of city he wanted: straight streets running 'uniform down to the water from the country bounds' and houses 'built upon a line' and every house placed in the 'middle of its plat, as to the breadth way of it, that so there may be ground on each side for gardens or orchards, or fields, that it may be a green country town, which will never be burned, and always be wholesome'. But his city was a social creation too: the derivation of Philadelphia from two words meaning 'love' and 'brother' suggests the ideal, and his declaration was simply that 'Mine eye is to a blessed government, and a virtuous, ingenuous and industrious society'.[4]

The utopian myth was also given practical form by the continuing tradition enshrined in monastic communities. The Jesuits, founded in 1540, maintained the monastic ideal and a particular form of community life, particularly in South America.

Concepts of ideal communities within the framework of a

universal dream of a perfect world or a golden age, and stimulated by known practical examples, were therefore well formed when the economic upheavals of the eighteenth century heralded the changing world of the industrial revolution, intellectuals offered new concepts of democracy and social equality, and a ground swell of humanitarianism gave new outlets for social conscience. Under these triple stimuli the nineteenth century formed a new breeding ground for new ideals and new visions, and the utopian heritage was to provide an important bedrock on which new philosophies were to be fashioned. Subsequent experiments following these speculations were in turn to become the birth pangs of an emergent town planning movement.

Utopia Interpreted

We have argued that in spite of important instances to the contrary, the impact of the Renaissance utopia was essentially that of a myth, whereby ideal social commonwealths were conceived in imaginary, far-off lands, the realization of which was highly unlikely. From the second half of the eighteenth century onwards, utopia was given an extended definition, and in the nineteenth century there was a new interpretation; the ideal state was now possible by social revolution and projects of social experiment could actively be taken up. Out of this dramatic change in outlook, a town planning movement, inheriting the mantle of earlier reformers, was to evolve.

The reasons for this realignment of utopian activity are complex, but we are helped in fully understanding the social traditions of town planning if we recognize three main elements: one, the impact of urban and industrial change; two, the religious and humanitarian backcloth of the age; and three, the political trend from oligarchy to democracy.

Urban events of the nineteenth century in Britain were quite without precedent; towns grew in size to an unparalleled degree, and settlements coalesced in continuous spreads, to be recognized by Geddes shortly after the turn of the century as conurbations. There was early hardship in urban life, especially amongst the most rapidly growing cities with an industrial base, and although material progress and individual betterment certainly occurred with a wide rise over the whole of society, endemic poverty and squalor remained to the end. In these circumstances it was inevitable that there should be agitation to improve man's lot in a period of bewildering change, to protect the weaker members of the community, to create order out of chaos and to abolish ugliness and seek beauty.

The rapidity of urban growth occasioned severe social complications; at first, especially, there was a lag in the creation of material resources necessary to meet the increase in population. Poverty, the battle for public health, the poor state of the country's towns, low housing standards, reduction in open space, the demands of industry, and the philosophy of the age which made it difficult for the worst effects to be withstood in any case; these were the issues of the Bleak Age, as the Hammonds described it.

It was the first half of the century that experienced the worst of the conditions. In 1790 the country labourers were about double the number of town workmen; in 1840 the town workmen were nearly double the country labourers. The cholera epidemic of 1832 turned public attention to the subject of the towns, and late in the 1830s and early in the 1840s a series of inquiries threw vivid light on urban conditions. There were no building restrictions to forestall overcrowding, and only in a few areas could enlightened landowners enforce certain town planning restrictions, as for example at Ashton under Lyne (Earl of Stamford), Huddersfield (Sir John Ramsden) and Glossop (Duke of Norfolk).

In spite of improvements on the situation of the early years, the century closed in a welter of social reports detailing the poverty and squalor of the time. Charles Booth's classic work, *The Life and Labour of the People of London*, revealed that forty per cent of the working class was contained in the three most depressed classes, 'the poor, the very poor and the lowest'. If Britain was not morally shocked, its military might was questioned when a large number of those enlisting for the Boer War were found unfit, weakened through years of inadequate living.

The economic character of the nineteenth century had marked social results during different decades. Hobsbawm[5] has drawn attention to the pattern of economic fluctuations and the nature of social movements during the century, suggesting that sudden expansions ('explosions' or 'leaps') in the size, strength and activity of social movements were closely linked with economic fluctuations of an industrial and capitalist economy. The first half of the century, at least up to 1848, saw widespread unrest typified by strikes. Luddite riots, farm labourer's risings, reform agitation, ten-hour campaigns, chartism and including radical community experiments. These agitations were closely linked with sudden increases in poverty at the bottom of economic slumps, when in the absence of trades unions sharp falls in earnings were inevitable.

The changing physical, economic and social conditions of the nineteenth century stimulated agitation and the growth of radical reform movements on many fronts. This was the situation, nourished by a utopian outlook, out of which stemmed an emergent town planning movement. A fundamental question was housing: better housing conditions, the design of workmen's cottages, the shame of slums and a slum environment, the reduction of housing densities, the provision of gardens, and overall health standards. All these were of course inseparable from wider issues such as the elimination of poverty and social degradation, the restoration of the dignity of the family and the individual, the provision of work, and encouragement of community life and the creation of healthy and beautiful cities: these were to give the town planning movement its all-embracing characteristic, extending its scope beyond that of purely a housing reform activity.

Another characteristic of the century, relevant to this development, was the evidence of humanitarianism. There was an evangelical revival of dynamic Christianity with a renewed social message, and this influenced a wide field of social activity. This was to give a particular stimulus to the activities of philanthropists in housing reform, manufacturers in improving living and working conditions, and reformers in exposing various social evils of the day. It was not enough that the century had its problems; it also needed people with conviction, driven by a concern for the well-being of the community for reform movements to gather pace and affect the conditions of the time.

In short, a key factor in the interpretation and realignment of utopian thought lay in the urban changes of the Industrial Revolution. The world was visibly being changed, and it became imperative to conceive of a different order of things without escaping in fictive imagination to the other side of the world. In this metamorphosis an important catalyst was to be a ground swell of humanitarianism which threw up vital figures in reform movements, who analysed conditions, exposed injustices, agitated for improvement and experimented with new possibilities.

An even more important instrument of change was political, associated with the stirrings towards democracy and social equality. Political revolutions indicated that the ideal state, far from being a myth, was now possible by social revolution, and events in America and particularly France at the end of the eighteenth century were to be especially important in securing changing attitudes.

In France, the first indications of the new tendencies were given by the Abbé Morelly, who developed the ideas of More and Campanella and propounded communistic theory. This was given in his *Basiliade*, published in 1753, which described the imaginary history of a people achieving perfectibility. He maintained that the corruption of man originated in the institution of private property and its protection by law, and this led him to recommend as a remedy for curing the social abuses of mid-eighteenth-century France absolute community of goods and to urge the uniformity of personal rights among all citizens.

Morelly's utopian dream was shared by Jean Jacques Rousseau and his doctrine of equality and many other powerful figures including Francis Noel Babeuf. The social ideal of the intellectuals became dignity of the individual, from which was to flow the equal rights of all in the eyes of the law, and the spirit of common brotherhood.

This spirit was not to be confined to France. In America, in the atmosphere of a newly secured independence, Thomas Paine, banished from his native England, produced his *Rights of Man* (1790). In this country William Godwin opposed the principle of private property and maintained his belief that environment was the main factor in the shaping of human conduct. The common possession of land was similarly urged by Thomas Spence and Charles Hall.

This new influence at the end of the eighteenth century has been suggested in some detail because it induced a vital, fresh element in socio-political thinking at this time. As we look for key factors in the positive application of utopian thinking, this is a period of great significance. The poets, Coleridge, Wordsworth and Southey provide important evidence.

We may recall that Wordsworth, in spite of the conservatism with which he is usually associated in later life, was in fact an ardent supporter of the French Revolution, until its excesses turned him away from support. On his walking tour through France, Italy and Switzerland in 1790 he saw the upheaval in full spate: 'O pleasant exercise of hope and joy!' begins his poem *The French Revolution*. The opportunity for recreating social order was now seen in very practical terms: achievements could be made here and now and did not rely on imaginary situations in some distant land. In Wordsworth's words the dreamers

Were called upon to exercise their skill,
Not in utopia, subterraneous Fields,
Or some secreted Island, Heaven knows where,
But in the very world which is the world
Of all of us, the place in which, in the end,
We find our happiness, or not at all.

These words mark an important watershed in time between abstract utopian thinking of the Renaissance writers and practical reform which was to be the characteristic of the nineteenth century. The stimulus was to be 'not in utopia . . . but in the very world which is the world of all of us'.

An immediate example was to be seen in the scheme of Samuel Taylor Coleridge for settling a small community in America at a place outside the range of government and untroubled by laws and taxes, an ideal which became known as Pantisocracy. The site was to be near Cooper's Town on the Susquehanna and the colony was to be communistic, with two to three hours' manual work a day from each man and other time devoted to study, discussion and enlightened education of children. The scheme took shape in Bristol in 1794 and was worked out in detail by a fellow poet, Robert Southey; even the design of the backwoodsmen's cottages was planned. But the project for twenty-six adventurers fizzled out in disillusionment and dissension between the parties. On this occasion theory was not realized, but the scene was set for a host of practical experiments and radical thinking.

Community Experiments

Pantisocracy was but a forerunner. Of much more importance were the ideas and achievements of Robert Owen in the first quarter of the nineteenth century. The main story is by now well known of how David Dale's cotton manufacturing village built at the Falls of Clyde in 1784 was made world-famous by his son-in-law Robert Owen. Bought in 1799 by Owen, the new company took over under the name of the New Lanark Twist Company, and he immediately reconstructed the whole establishment. He aimed to make New Lanark not merely an efficient factory but a well-governed human community based on his ideals. In achieving this he kept a tremendous hold over his employees, their houses and their shops; he ruled over the entire community as well as the factory. As a social experiment it deserves the deepest study; we cannot do more here than review briefly the broad details, but it is the principle underlying Owen's work that is important for the town planner. Owen considered that by altering the conditions under which the inhabitants worked and lived, the character and disposition of the people would gradually be improved. To achieve this, his idealism combined the rigour of both More and Plato.

His immediate schemes of social reform were comprehensive. Housing accommodation was increased from one to two rooms, and insanitary ashpits were removed from the front of buildings. There were daily sweepings of the streets and lectures were given on house cleanliness; a committee was set up to inspect families and report on household conditions. Watchmen were appointed to combat drunkenness. The village store was reorganized on a co-operative principle and a savings bank and a benefit society were set up.

Owen succeeded in getting his work people to submit to this system of registration of character. His New Institution was opened in 1816, to be used exclusively for school classes, church, lectures, concerts and recreation. The integration of educational and social reform was made manifest. Small wonder that New Lanark became a centre of attraction, with 20,000 visitors between 1815 and 1825 including statesmen, philanthropists, bishops, foreign princes, dukes and ambassadors.

But Owen's social solutions did not stop there. To combat the rising problem of unemployment after Waterloo Owen put forward a series of comprehensive recommendations including training and instruction, amelioration of working conditions, and the creation of an establishment housing a population of between 1,000 and 1,500 persons. He conceived a two-storey block of buildings grouped round a large open quadrangle with a range of buildings in the centre forming two parallelograms. These were his 'agricultural and manufacturing villages of unity and mutual co-operation', dismissed by his critics as 'parallelograms of paupers'.

The form of Owen's proposal was reminiscent of that of the French architect, Claude Nicolas Ledoux, who was responsible for the design of Chaux, a town for salt workers, dating from 1776. His first plan was for a quadrangle of buildings (comprising workers' homes, common buildings and allotment gardens) arranged as a 1,000-foot square; later revisions changed the square to an ellipse and finally a semi-ellipse.

Owen's proposal was amended somewhat in the *Report to the County of Lanark* (1820). The communities were now thought of as agricultural villages, but the benevolent despotism of his ideals was retained. For example, food was to be prepared at a cooking centre and the inhabitants were to dine as one family. They were even to be clothed in the distinctive dress of highland garb. The affairs of the community were to be conducted by a committee composed of members between forty and fifty years old.

It was no doubt easy to dismiss these proposals as unworkable, and indeed Owen's subsequent practical experiments were in fact failures. (His colony at New Harmony in the United States bought in 1824 had to be closed four years later. Similarly his Queenwood [Hampshire] experiment in 1839 was not successful, breaking up in 1846 after quarrels between working class Socialists and Owen's wealthier supporters.) But Owen's exploits and writings are stimulating, and the comprehensiveness of his vision is compelling. His *New View of Society* should be read for his views on the formation of human character and the application of the principle to practice. The very title of his *Report to the County of Lanark* in 1820 illustrates the totality of his concern: 'Report to the County of Lanark, of a Plan for relieving public distress and removing discontent, by giving permanent productive employment to the poor and working classes, under arrangements which will essentially improve their character, and ameliorate their condition, diminish the expenses of production and consumption, and create markets coextensive with production.'

Throughout the whole of the nineteenth century a common theme in the Owenite tradition was the setting up of communities in new settlements. Religious persecution and the desire for freedom of expression had given a long tradition of this particular solution, especially in North America where there had been settlements by such as the Moravians, Quakers and Philadelphians. Nineteenth-century Britain was to throw up a continuous series of new secular experiments precisely on these lines for communities of a particular social outlook or persuasion.

A certain characteristic thread runs through them. They were usually practical experiments *de novo* in settings removed from the society and environment of the 'outside' world. To this extent they represented the escapist ideal in the utopian tradition; they were community experiments designed for the people who were to be members of that community; they were only indirectly leavens to total society. Furthermore, in the nineteenth century at any rate they were often associated with a return to the land; to this extent they were regressive in outlook in the face of industrialism. The colonies were run on tightly knit community lines, many at least 'co-operative' in nature and many frankly communistic. Lastly, they were marred by fractious disputes, financial ruin and, except for a handful of cases, destined for a brief life in spite of (or perhaps because of?) the intense idealism and enthusiasm of their founders.

The individual stories have been well documented but each deserves study because they contribute so much to an understanding of the more realistically based community ventures, such as those of the soap and chocolate magnates later in the century. A prerequisite of course was the particular vision of the founder. Enthusiasm and drive were fundamental for any success, and this was rarely achieved for long periods.

The close-knit features of these communities was a common characteristic. Many colonies were run on co-operative lines even before the Rochdale movement began in 1844. At the end of the century the colonies of Tolstoy and his disciples, and anarchists such as Kropotkin, still showed the desire for communities of small, self-supporting units.

The larger colonies were on Owenite lines with concern for the arrangement of buildings or their design. John Minter Morgan's 'Christian Commonwealth', for example, involved a scheme for self-supporting villages with the inhabitants housed in four-roomed cottages in the centre of a thousand acres of land. On the other hand Fourier's proposal was for a *phalanstère* for 1,620 people, a scheme taken up with the Brook Farm experiment in the United States.

Each of these community experiments represented the aspirations and idealism of groups of people with a vision for a new society and anxiety or despair about the old. The Chartist Land Plan of Feargus O'Connor was in many ways a typical example, driven on by powerful emotions, but in the end abortive. He urged land reform, considering that smallholdings cultivated by spade husbandry would in themselves be profitable and that the land would encourage independence and self-reliance. The Chartist Co-operative Land Company was formed in 1846 and there were 70,000 members scattered over the country. O'Connor himself undertook the work of buying estates and preparing them for settlement. There was the enormous task of raising capital, but there was no denying his vision. 'If those with money to lend

B

would lend it,' he declared, 'I would change the whole face of society in twelve months from this day. I would make a paradise of England in less than five years.'[6] Estates were bought and others planned, but in the end only about 250 members of his National Land Company succeeded in getting allotments. His estates such as O'Connorville and Charterville came to nothing.

Later in the century General Booth's *In Darkest England and the Way Out* (1890) described the lot of the homeless, the workless and the destitute of Britain at that time—the submerged tenth. Booth had his own solution, and again it was in the form of colonies. His scheme consisted of 'the formation of these people [unemployed] into self-helping and self-sustaining communities, each being a kind of co-operative society, or partriarchal family, governed and disciplined on the principles which have already proved so effective in the Salvation Army.'[7]

His communities were to form three types: the city colony, the farm colony and the oversea colony. He also proposed the establishment of a series of industrial settlements or suburban villages of perhaps 1,000–2,000 dwellings in each, in rural areas. A number of colonies was established, particularly in Essex, to add to the many experiments of the century.

Others with solutions for social reform were literary idealists rather than practical exponents. Occasionally however some writers were activists themselves. Kropotkin's *Field, Factories and Workshops* (1898), for example, expressed the philosophy of his free village communities, and Theodore Hertzka's *Freeland: A Social Anticipation* (1890) led to the founding of the International Freeland Society and his colony in East Africa. Similarly Ebenezer Howard's own book *Tomorrow: A Peaceful Path to Real Reform* (1898) anticipated his practical work at Letchworth.

In other cases a man's writing led to others taking up his ideals. Etienne Cabet, for example, was a journalist and an unsuccessful politician who had propounded his views in *Voyage en Icarie* in 1838. His own community experiments at Nauvoo near St Louis failed and further work was left to his disciples after his death. Similarly, Fourier's proposals concerning *phalanstères* were taken up after his death, and it was left to Channing, an American, to recommend Fourierism to colonies such as at Brook Farm, mentioned previously. Fourier's book *Association Domestique Agricole* was to promote more than thirty *phalanstères* in America, all many years after his death in 1835.

Propagandists for Urban Form

But there were other reformers and visionaries who preferred to encourage the direction of thought towards ideal communities through literary efforts rather than practical experiment. Their message was for others to take up. James Silk Buckingham in the middle of the century may be given as an example. His book *National Evils and Practical Remedies* was published in 1849. In this he proposed the formation of a company to be:

> The Model Town Association, for the purpose of building an entirely New Town, to combine within itself every advantage of beauty, security, healthfulness and convenience, that the latest discoveries in architecture and science can confer upon it; and which should at the same time, be peopled by an adequate number of inhabitants, with such due proportions between the agricultural and manufacturing classes, and between the possessors of capital skill and labour, as to produce by the new combinations and discipline under which its code of rules and regulations might place the whole body, the highest degree of abundance in every necessity of life, and many luxuries, united with the lightest amount of labour and care, and the highest degree of health, contentment, morality and enjoyment, yet seen in any existing community, established on the principles by which society is now generally regulated.[8]

Buckingham's Model Town Victoria (Plates I and II) was both a carefully detailed physical plan as well as a social plan; it was never acted upon but at least it incorporated ideas which were taken up by later innovators. Physically, the town was to be built in a series of concentric squares building up to a mile square with a population not to exceed 10,000, with eight main radial avenues. The plan 'unites the greatest degree of order, symmetry, space and healthfulness, in the largest supply of air and light, and in the most perfect system of drainage, with the comfort and convenience of all classes'. Confident of success, Buckingham declared that his town 'inhabited by a well organized community . . . would banish nearly all the evils of disease, vice, crime, poverty, misery and hostile and antagonistic feelings, from amongst its members; and produce a larger amount of happiness than is possible to be obtained by the great mass of mankind, according to the defective and ill-organized arrangements of the present state of society'.

This social utopia was to be accomplished on very much Owenite lines: the imposition of selective criteria according to the ideals of the founder. There were to be no intoxicants, weapons of war and tobacco. There was to be freedom of religious opinions, but the Sabbath was to be kept sacred to devotion. No women were to be employed in 'laborious occupations' and no child was to be employed in any kind of labour 'unsuited to its age and strength'. Every dwelling was to have a w.c. and public baths were to be provided 'at convenient distances in each quarter of the Town'. There were to be communal restaurants and children were to be trained in nursery schools. There was to be free medical assistance and free education up to fifteen. There was to be 'the most perfect apparatus to be applied for consuming smoke' and all unsuitable buildings 'such as abbatoirs' were to be located away from residence and workshops.

These and many other injunctions indicate Buckingham's approach to the planning of ideal communities. His role was that of a benevolent dictator who framed rules for society within the context of a physical plan. He went further than Owen by conceiving a total system not for a factory community or even a parallelogram, but for communities of 10,000 persons. Indeed, as the total population increased home colonies were proposed formed from the parent city. By this means 'in less than a century, all the least peopled parts of England, Scotland, Ireland and Wales, might be progressively covered'.

Of other literary idealists Robert Pemberton, for example, in *The Happy Colony* (1854) proposed a Model Town in New Zealand, Queen Victoria Town. As another example, Benjamin Ward Richardson conceived *Hygeia, a City of Health* (1876). This was a model city itemized in detail from the health and arrangement point of view, and to this extent he foresaw the tremendous technical improvements which were to benefit town development. 'Utopia itself is but another word for time,' he declared confidently, 'and some day the masses, who heed us not, or smile incredulously at our proceedings, will awake to our conceptions.'

An additional impetus to a new vision of the possibilities of urban life came from an artistic source, propagated by the novelist, the aesthete and the architect. As an antidote to an age of industrial ugliness William Morris, for example, founded the Arts and Craft movement with the intention of ensuring good design by making the individual craftsman conscious of his own responsibilities. He founded his own firm in 1861 to produce wallpapers, furniture, tapestries and even stained-glass windows, but perhaps he had his greatest and certainly his most popular impact as a novelist. In *News From Nowhere* (1890) he envisaged the coming socialist society and depicted the new world that might result. His narrative theme 'the sleeper awakes' had been adapted two years earlier by Edward Bellamy in *Looking Backwards*, another popular book of the day; Julian West of Boston had fallen asleep to awake in A.D. 2000 to find a much-improved city.

Morris described the dream of one William Guest in a shabby Thames-side London suburb, during which we are asked to imagine, as one instance, a Thames waterman: '. . . nothing rough or coarse about him, and clean as might be. His dress was not like any modern work-a-day clothes I had seen, but would have served very well as a costume for a picture of fourteenth-century life: it was of dark blue cloth, simple enough but of fine web, and without a stain on it. . . . In short, he seemed like some specially manly and refined young gentleman.'[9]

Morris looked to the guild movement to alleviate the soullessness of industrial society, founding three guilds, the Century Guild (1882), the Art Workers Guild (1884) and the Arts and Crafts Exhibition Society (1888). John Ruskin had similar leanings and we should not forget his influence. He founded the Guild of St George, with the aim of purchasing land for labourers and for reviving agriculture. An experiment was undertaken at Totley, near Sheffield.

But the teaching of Ruskin and Morris was associated with a wider concern for the drabness of nineteenth-century towns, and in the closing years of the century this was to be a most powerful influence on the evolution of the town planning movement. It is not a specifically 'social' influence in the way that other aspects have been described, but it is bound up with social fulfilment and the very nature of life in towns, and therefore is very relevant to this review.

Morris himself in *News From Nowhere* had shown concern for townscape. The known evils of Thames-side had disappeared: 'The soap works with their smoke-vomiting chimneys were gone; the engineer's works gone; the leadworks gone; and no sound of rivetings or hammering came down the west wind from Thorneycroft's.' But there was positive improvement too, for example the buildings at Hammersmith market: 'This whole mass of architecture . . . was not only exquisitely beautiful in itself, but it bore upon it the expression of such generosity and abundance of life that I was exhilarated to a pitch that I had never yet reached.'

At about the same time, in May 1899, a small volume of essays was published in Vienna entitled *City Planning according to Artistic Principles* in which Camillo Sitte analysed the civic and artistic character of Old European towns. He abstracted from their layout a series of principles on which city planning might be restored to an artistic basis, and illustrated this with reference mainly to Vienna and the new Ringstrasse development. There was clearly an increasing awareness for improvement in town design: 'The modern city planner has become poverty stricken as far as art is concerned,' he wrote.

Morris had formed the Society for the Protection of Ancient Buildings in 1877, and Octavia Hill battled ceaselessly for open space in the metropolitan area. The architect W. R. Lethaby was one of a number to take up this striving for improvement and relate it to the art of town building. In a lecture in 1897 he gave his views on contemporary London.

> . . . I must confess that my heart fails me at the enormous-ness—the enormity—of it. A half hundred square miles, once wood and cornland, roofed over, where we grow sickly like grass under a stone, intersected by interminable avenues all asphalt, lamp posts, pipes and wires: a coil of underground labyrinth which Dante might have added to his world of torment—the Inner Circle: a gloomy sky above, from which falls a sticky slime of soot: public pageantry reduced to the two shows of the 5th and 9th of November: gardens which seem to imitate stamped zinc—such are the characteristics of modern London.[10]

But like Sitte, Lethaby could make positive proposals. He urged, for example, the creation of a wide pedestrian way from Waterloo Bridge to the British Museum, an embankment on the South Bank and an improvement of central railway stations. He also urged a dividing off of London from non-London, suggesting a zone embracing Richmond Park, Putney and Wimbledon as a belt of 'fruitful garden ground'. Once again there was the clear view that the social problems of the large city could be met by limitations on size. 'A new and better London,' he said, 'can only be completed as old Rome was founded—by turning a plough trench round it.'

Housing Reform and Model Communities

As the nineteenth century progressed, housing reform increasingly went hand in hand with social reform. This stimulated concern not with theory about the structure of ideal communities or even with their establishment and management, but with tackling in a practical way the housing evils of the day.

Philanthropic housing associations were emerging by the mid-nineteenth century. For example, the Metropolitan Association for Improving the Dwellings of the Industrious Classes was formed in 1841 and the Society for the Improvement of the Condition of the Labouring Classes in 1843. A number of London associations and societies were formed and their success was copied in the provinces, notably Leeds, Manchester, Bristol and Newcastle. Most prominent however were the Peabody Trust (1862), founded by George Peabody, and the Improved Industrial Dwellings Company, founded by Sir Sydney Waterlow in 1863. Later, Octavia Hill was to be instrumental in the founding of Kyrle Society(1877) in Glasgow.

But the improvements which took place for the working classes through the medium of voluntary associations and through state reform were insufficient, and it required a host of experiments by the industrial magnates of the time to show more dramatic results. The theme of model dwellings was to be taken up and emphasized in scale by the creation of philanthropists' villages.

The first model villages were clustered in the wool and worsted manufacturing centres in the West Riding. Their distinguishing feature was that they were conceived and executed by benefactors who were factory owners: Sir Titus Salt's Saltaire near Bradford, Colonel Edward Akroyd with his Copley and Akroydon (Halifax) and John, Joseph and Sir Francis Crossley with the development of their West Hill Park area of Halifax. This constituted the Bradford–Halifax School of model village builders.

Of these, the Saltaire experiment was the most notable. Salt moved his mill from Bradford to a 25-acre site outside the city on the Midland railway and the Leeds–Liverpool canal, close to the River Aire. He commissioned Mawson and Lockwood, a firm of Bradford achitects, to build a model village for the 3,000 textile operatives employed in his works, which manufactured the bulk of the world's alpaca cloth. Eight hundred and fifty houses and 45 alms houses were built. The cottages were mainly of a type with a parlour, kitchen, pantry and two bedrooms. They mostly had a small, flagged back-yard, an ashpit, an outside privy and a cellar. There were churches, baths, a public wash-house, a village institute, shops, a park and a hospital. The ideal village was almost completed before Salt's death in 1876, but increasingly the concept of an ideal industrial community in a rural setting was lost as a flood of speculative building surrounded the site.

Outside the West Riding another example of a model village was at Bromborough Pool on the Wirral peninsula developed by Price's Patent Candle Company. New works were built in 1853 and housing development followed with cottages laid out in short terraces with wide spaces between each block and ample gardens at the back as well as the front.

These examples reflected a very large number of such experiments on the Continent and in America. In Germany, the Krupp family in 1865 began the first of several model villages, and there were workers' colonies also in France, Italy and Holland. In America the Pullman development near Chicago between 1880 and 1884 is perhaps the best known.

In England, Port Sunlight, Bournville, Earswick and Hull Garden Village were the most notable experiments at about the turn of the century. These were more than industrialists' housing schemes; they were model towns and the forerunners of the garden city experiment. But they truly belong to the social reform movement because their designers saw them as contributing both to the alleviation of poor housing and environmental conditions in larger towns as well as to the positive creation of happy communities. These experiments have been well documented, but perhaps we can usefully remind ourselves of the circumstances of one of the better-known ones, Bournville.

In Birmingham the Cadbury brothers transferred their factory in 1880 from Bridge Street in the city to a green field site four miles to the south-west. This in itself was an act of some courage for there were some immediate disadvantages, not the least remoteness from the supply of labour. This was overcome when terms were made with the railway company which secured cheap weekly tickets for workmen from Birmingham.

A number of workers' houses were built, but it was not until later that this particular aspect of the development took place. Alive to the housing reform movement, Cadbury began by purchasing 120 acres in the neighbourhood of the works, an area gradually increased to 842 acres including the property of the firm. The layout of the estate began in 1895. Cadbury ensured that each house had a suitable garden and that no building occupied more than a quarter of the curtilage. The roads were tree-lined and one-tenth of the land (in addition to roads and gardens) was reserved for parks and recreation grounds; indeed, Bournville began with a village green, two parks, and two playgrounds quite apart from the school playgrounds. Welfare schemes, the provision of a village institute and Ruskin Hall for the Adult School movement added to the amenities and facilities of the estate to meet the needs of a happy community.

All the evidence shows that Cadbury was extremely successful as a philanthropist at Bournville. As a social experiment it attracted international attention just as Owen's New Lanark community had done at the beginning of the century. The provision of working class homes to an almost unprecedented standard, good industrial conditions and a level of high wages were there for all to see. It was to be even claimed that there was a consequence upon human health and physique. Twelve years after the beginning of the estate a comparison was made between the height and weight of children at Bournville and those of the Floodgate Street area of Birmingham. At every age from six to twelve years the Bournville children were heavier by several pounds.

Ebenezer Howard

The garden city experiments at Port Sunlight and Bournville were the direct antecedents of Ebenezer Howard's own work at Letchworth, itself preceded by his book *Tomorrow: a Peaceful Path to Real Reform* (1898), reissued with slight revisions in 1902 as *Garden Cities of Tomorrow*. Particular attention should be paid to this work as the culmination of a century-long movement in community experiments, for although the garden city was a physical solution to urban problems it also expressed social ideals for long enshrined in the goals surrounding the concept of ideal communities.

Howard's immense contribution was that he assimilated the contributions made by a number of theorists and experimentalists, both contemporary and previous to his day, and reinterpreted the social theme to meet the needs of the time. Born in 1850, he had no special advantage of class or education, but on returning to England from America he was to move amongst nonconformist churchmen and reformers concerned with the land question. He had many particular influences upon him, including Bellamy's novel *Looking Backward,* Buckingham's Model Town, and proposals for the organized migratory movement of population from London put forward by Edward Gibbon Wakefield in his *Art of Colonization* (1849) and later by Alfred Marshall.

Howard's starting point was the spectacle of overcrowded cities and the depopulation of rural areas. He wrote:

> Whatever may have been the causes which have operated in the past, and are operating now, to draw the people into the cities, those causes may all be summed up as 'attractions'; and it is obvious, therefore, that no remedy can possibly be effective which will not present to the people, or at least to considerable portions of them, greater 'attractions' than our cities now possess, so that the force of the old 'attractions' shall be overcome by the force of new 'attractions' which are to be created.[11]

This allowed Howard to develop his concept of 'magnets'. 'There are in reality not only . . . two alternatives—town life and country life—but a third alternative, in which all the advantages of the most energetic and active town life, with all the beauty and delight of the country may be secured in perfect combination.' His now famous 'three magnets' depicted Town and Country with their advantages and corresponding drawbacks, while the merits of Town–Country were shown to be free from the disadvantages of either.

Howard's solution does not require lengthy restatement. His concept of the satellite community called for the provision of a permanent belt of open land to be used for agriculture; the physical spread of the city was to be limited; there was to be municipal ownership, and the town was to be self-supporting by its own industry. He postulated a Garden City of 30,000 population built near to the centre of 6,000 acres; it was to be of circular form, three-quarters of a mile from centre to circumference. Six wide boulevards acted as radials dividing the city into six equal parts or wards. Five and a half acres in the centre was to be a garden containing the larger public buildings. Parks and various land uses, residential and industrial, were to be found in concentric rings (Plates III and IV).

These were the physical details, but the vision and social idealism of the reformer was expressed too. 'Town and country must be married,' Howard declared, 'and out of this joyous union will spring a new hope, a new life, a new civilisation.' The means of the exercise may have been the physical creation of a new town, but the end or objective was social: 'to raise the standard of health and comfort of all true workers of whatever grade—the means by which these objects are to be achieved being a healthy, natural and economic combination of town and country life. . . .'

Howard was a social realist; he was not the benevolent director of earlier communities nor even the enlightened philanthropist of workers' model settlements. To this extent his contribution to the evolution of the town planning movement was an important step forward. He recognized that, 'Probably the chief cause of failure in former social experiments has been a misconception of the principal element in the problem—human nature itself. The degree of strain which average human nature will bear in an altruistic direction has not been duly considered by those who have essayed the task of suggesting new forms of social organization.'

Howard was as much concerned for free enterprise as for social control. This was expressed in the varied architecture of his postulated Garden City, where 'fullest measure of individual taste and preference is encouraged'. He appreciated that earlier schemes were rigid concepts which mistrusted the value of individual effort. The significance of Howard is that he took a major advance by acknowledging the importance of recognizing social needs and of providing the opportunity to meet them. 'Among the greatest needs of man and of society today,' he wrote, 'as at all times, are these: a worthy aim and opportunity to realise it; work and ends worth working for. All that a man is, and all that he may become, is summed up in his aspirations, and this is no less true of society than of the individual.'

Shortly after the publication of *Tomorrow* the Garden City Association was formed; a pioneer company was registered and in 1903 a rural site of more than 3,800 acres was purchased at Letchworth. The garden city movement had begun in earnest, and this particularly British contribution to world planning was to flower in the new towns of post-war years.

The social basis of garden cities was not to be forgotten. Raymond Unwin, who expressed Howard's aims in practice and who was much influenced by William Morris, expressed his philosophy thus:

Hitherto our modern towns have been too much mere aggregations of people; but it must be our work to transform these aggregations into consciously organized communities, finding in their towns and cities new homes in the true sense, enjoying that fuller life which comes from more intimate intercourse, and finding in the organization of their town scope and stimulus for the practice and development of the more noble aims which have contributed to bring them together.[12]

In a sense it may be said that the social theme of town planning as a comprehensive view of society and environment has scarcely advanced or developed since then. The social upheavals of the nineteenth century died away as the worst of the injustices and urban degradations were removed. The experiments of colonies and ideal communities passed. The idealism of social agitators was channelled into other directions such as politics and industrial agitation; social reform was seen on a different front.

But the social theme remained linked with the planning movement through the common medium of housing and its improvement. The moralistic view about environmental improvement, and the consequences which might stem from it, was a common credence at the very beginning of town planning. Mr John Burns, President of the Local Government Board, in debating the Housing, Town Planning etc. Bill in its passage through Parliament in 1908 could say that the object of the bill was 'to provide a domestic condition for the people in which their physical health, their morals, their character and their whole social condition can be improved. . . .'[13]

The emphasis on housing and the social improvements which better housing could effect characterized the early years of this century. Quite understandably the cry was for greater space around dwellings. Two prominent examples of the day were the Hampstead Garden Suburb, developed at eight houses to the acre, and the Harborne (Birmingham) Garden Suburb at the equivalent of nine and a quarter houses to the acre. Air and sunlight were the new prized amenities.

Britain of course was by no means the only country in which there was protest against poor housing conditions. For example in America there was the crusade against congested tenements, which led to the Tenement House Act of 1901. Organizations were formed for the purpose of building better housing for the low-income worker, and as the 'city beautiful' concept swept the country the seeds of town planning were planted.

We should remember however that the relationship of the social theme to planning was not only through housing in the narrow sense of provision of better houses. It was certainly concerned with the improvement of living conditions, but this was also to be achieved in a more indirect way, namely the fight against suburban development (particularly of Greater London) and the ever-increasing size of cities. Howard's solution for optimum social arrangements was indeed eminently suited to the problems of a rapidly expanding metropolis and uncontrolled suburban spread. The outer ring of Greater London suburbs grew by about fifty per cent in each of the three intercensal periods between 1861 and 1891 and forty-five per cent in the last decade of the century. The 1909 Act offered at least the possibility of controlling the spread of London and the big cities by giving permissive powers for local authorities to prepare schemes for land in course of development or likely to be used for building purposes, 'to ensure that . . in the future land in the vicinity of towns should be developed to secure proper sanitary conditions and amenity and convenience in the laying out of the land itself'.

Twentieth-Century Developments

We have seen in this chapter how the town planning movement emerged from a body of thought and practical experiment centred round man in his social and physical environment. Underlying the events of the nineteenth century, and giving them coherence, was the bedrock of utopian idealism. Beyond this, some thought progress to be achieved only through revolution and the overthrow of the present order; some, more practically, through escapism to found colonies either in this country or abroad in new settings. As the century developed others saw real progress in the creation of new communities to exist side by side with the old order, presenting examples for adoption as an ideal; others worked on the patient erosion of injustices or inadequacies and sought to improve standards in public health or housing. Later, others demanded new leisure facilities such as open space, or rediscovered the art in town building to present society with a worthy setting for the conduct of human affairs. Finally, there was to be the demand for the public control of land use and the manner in which land was to be developed. These were the strands in the evolution of town planning.

The nineteenth century was a period of unparalleled social change, population growth and urban development. The twentieth is likewise a unique period and our big cities are spawning new problems. But the urban characteristics of the two centuries are very different. In the last century towns were basically attractive, in the sense that concentrating forces were at work in confining urban spread; the present century on the other hand has seen an increasing tendency for populations to leave inner areas for outer areas and suburbs. Centrifugal forces have been replaced by centripetal.

It is significant that the year of publication of *Tomorrow* coincided with the first experiments in electric traction and wth the beginnings of the petrol motor, and these new forms of transport ushered in an era of urban expansion which Wells might foresee but Howard could not allow for. Consequently, both the urban condition and the urban proletariat at the present day are quite different from the time of Owen, O'Connor or Cadbury.

But in many ways the problem is precisely the same. Man has the technical capacity to construct or redevelop cities; he has the aesthetic ability to give them livable qualities; but he still has to prove that he can provide for mass society a physical, economic and social environment which promotes satisfaction and where individual lives and personalities benefit from mutual contact and from the maximum provision of opportunities and choice.

It is during the last 100 years that this problem has come to a head: in this period the urban population has come to outnumber the rural population, large towns and cities now exist on an unprecedented scale, and a distinctive urban proletariat has been created. Old solutions are no longer adequate. We are no longer concerned with the search for 'ideal communities', or even perhaps with the search for 'community', although the underlying idealism may be an important motivating force. The turning point was undoubtedly in the era of the model towns and garden cities, for in these experiments the search for happy communities became fully integrated in the process of town building.

But from this point, town planning from the social aspect has in a sense made little progress. During the twentieth century an advance in social planning has usually seemed to rely on the creation of new urban forms.

As an early example, the idealization of the industrial city was expressed by a young French architect, Tony Garnier, while a student in the years 1901–4; his work was published in 1917. He designed a hypothetical industrial town, called simply *Cité Industrielle*, with an imaginary site, comprising a plateau with high land to the north and a valley and a river to the south. The plateau was to be used for residential purposes and the valley for the factories for which power was to be derived from a local hydroelectric station. The total population, including an imaginary existing old town, was to be about 32,000. It has been argued[14] that the social content of the *Cité Industrielle* has to be seen in the context of Emile Zola's literary counterpart, *Travail*, written contemporaneously with the planning of the *Cité*, and based on the early socialist utopian doctrines of Fourier. Garnier omitted churches and introduced building necessary for the syndicates required by the socialist form of government.

As another example, Le Corbusier poured scorn on the garden city, and postulated his own creation. His attitude was typified with the remark that, 'suburban life is a despicable delusion entertained by a society stricken with blindness'. Or again: 'Suburbs are broken dislocated limbs! The city has been torn apart and scattered in meaningless fragments across the countryside. What is the point of life in such places? How are people to live in them?' His solution of course was to create the Radiant City, 'three to six times greater than the idealistic, ruinous and inoperative figures recommended by urban authorities still imbued with romantic ideology'.[15] Here, the pedestrian would never meet a vehicle, and all sporting activities would take place directly outside people's homes in the midst of parks, trees, lawns and lakes.

In exactly the same way, but with a very different solution, Frank Lloyd Wright rejected the city: 'like some hopelessly inadequate old boat or building, the city itself is still in use, inhabited because we feel we cannot afford to throw it away and allow the spirit of Time, Place and Man to build the new ones we have so much need'.[16] He envisaged Broadacre City, where no less than one acre was to be allotted to each individual man, woman and child. His dream was that 'when democracy triumphs and builds the great new city, no man will live as a servile or savage animal; holing in or trapped in some cubicle or an upended extension of some narrow street'.

This search for the creation of new forms to redress the balance of the old found powerful expression in the garden city movement (Welwyn was to follow Letchworth), the concept of satellite towns, the New Towns of post-war Britain and contemporary flirtations with linear cities, echoing the work of Soria y Mata in 1882 in Madrid. Almost as social laboratories these were to be the new important areas for social planning. On the other hand it is true that the neighbourhood concept for planning strategy was as applicable to old towns as well as new, but there again the first practical expressions were obviously to be found in areas of new development.

There were of course good reasons for pinning faith on new urban forms. The Geddesian influence which saw specific stages in the rise and fall of a city was strong. We may recall the five periods: polis, the early city; metropolis, the large but healthy city; megalopis, the unhealthy oversized city; parasitopolis, the parasitic city; and pathopolis, the diseased, shrinking, dying city.[17] This was a view suggested by Mumford who saw the sequence: metropolis, megalopis, tyrannopolis and necropolis, the dying city.[18]

It is difficult however to draw a parallel between the development of an urban culture and the flowering, maturing and death of an organism. There is no evidence to suppose that a city will have such a life cycle. But this was a popular view and it has perhaps been instrumental in turning planners' attention away from the traditional city to pin faith and hope in new urban fancies, and to see them as the settings for happier communities. This is not to deny that new urban forms may be needed, but the traditional city is still with us and the bulk of the urban population will continue to live there for the foreseeable future. Contemporary problems are concentrated there, and awareness of them has come from the accelerated process of planned renewal in most of our cities.

The remainder of the century may see new experiments in urban form, even to the extent of creation of new cities. But the great force of attention is going to be on existing towns and their problems. The opportunities for redefining the social content of town planning have therefore entered a new phase, when in the maturing of the planning movement, concern for communities everywhere can be made manifest. Our knowledge of the urban and social systems is still slender, but we can be assured of the complex interrelationship of the social, physical and economic environment. Town planning is now in the position of making a maximum contribution to the development and redevelopment of our cities. A realistic interpretation of planning's social theme to meet the needs of the age will enhance that contribution for the benefit of 'the great city, the mother of culture, the birthplace of freedom and justice, the glittering playground of life, man's world of stone without which he, for better or for worse, in lowliness or exaltation, would never have become what he is now'.[19]

REFERENCES TO CHAPTER 1

1. F. Haverfield, *Ancient Town Planning*, Oxford University Press, 1913.
2. Lewis Mumford, *The Story of Utopias—Ideal Commonwealths and Social Myths*, Harrap, 1923.
3. J. H. Lupton, *The Utopia of Sir Thomas More*, first edition of Ralph Robynson's Translation in 1551, Oxford, 1895.
4. Catherine Owens Peare, *William Penn*, Dennis Dobson, London, 1956.
5. E. J. Hobsbawm, 'Economic Fluctuations and Some Social Movements Since 1800', *The Economic History Review*, Second Series Vol. V, No. 1, 1952.
6. Joy MacAskill, 'The Chartist Land Plan', in *Chartist Studies*, editor Asa Briggs, Macmillan, 1959.
7. General Booth, *In Darkest England and the Way Out*, London, 1890.
8. James S. Buckingham, *National Evils and Practical Remedies*, London, 1849.
9. William Morris, *Stories in Prose, Stories in Verse, Shorter Poems, Lectures and Essays*, editor G. D. H. Cole, Nonesuch Press, 1944.
10. W. R. Lethaby, *Of Beautiful Cities*, London, 1897.
11. Ebenezer Howard, *Garden Cities of Tomorrow*, editor F. J. Osborn, Faber & Faber, 1946.
12. Raymond Unwin, *Town Planning in Practice*, Ernest Benn, 1909.
13. Quoted in J. B. Cullingworth, *Town and Country Planning in England and Wales*, Allen & Unwin, 1967.
14. Dora Wiebenson, 'Utopian Aspects of Tony Garnier's Cité Industrielle', *Society of Architectural Historians' Journal*, Vol. 19, 1960.
15. Le Corbusier, *The Radiant City*, 1964. (*La Ville Radieuse*, 1933.)
16. Frank Lloyd Wright, *The Living City*, Horizon Press, New York, 1958.
17. P. Geddes, *Cities in Evolution*, London, 1915.
18. Lewis Mumford, *The Culture of Cities*, London, 1938.
19. Wolf Schneider, *Babylon is Everywhere* (trans.), Hodder & Stoughton, 1963.

GENERAL BIBLIOGRAPHY TO CHAPTER 1

Patrick Abercrombie, *Town and Country Planning*, third edition, revised by D. Rigby Childs, Oxford University Press, 1959.
W. H. G. Armytage, *Heavens Below: Utopian Experiments in England, 1560–1960*, Routledge, 1961.
W. Ashworth, *The Genesis of Modern British Town Planning*, Routledge, 1954.
M. Beer, *Socialist Struggles and Modern Socialism* (trans.), H. J. Stemming, revised, 1925.

E. Moberley Bell, *Octavia Hill*, Constable, 1946.
L. Benevolo, *The Origins of Modern Town Planning* (trans.), Routledge, 1967.
Marie Louise Berneri, *Journey Through Utopia*, Routledge, 1950.
Paul Bloomfield, *Imaginary Worlds or the Evolution of Utopias*, London, 1932.
Asa Briggs, *A Study of the Work of Seebohm Rowntree, 1871–1954*, Longmans, 1961.
Gordon E. Cherry, 'The Spirit and Purpose of Town Planning: A Historical Approach', *Journal of the Town Planning Institute*, Vol. 55, No. 1, January 1969.
G. Kitson Clark, *The Making of Victorian England*, Methuen, 1962.
Norman Cohn, *The Pursuit of the Millennium*, Secker & Warburg, London, 1957.
G. D. H. Cole, *A History of Socialist Thought, Vol. I, The Forerunners, 1789–1850*, Macmillan, 1959.
G. R. and C. C. Collins, *Camillo Sitte and the Birth of Modern City Planning*, Phaidon Press, 1965.
Walter L. Creese, *The Search for Environment*, Yale University Press, 1966.
Alex Cullen, *Adventures in Socialism*, John Smith, Glasgow, 1910.
Rosa Druiff, 'Saltaire: Pioneer Factory Village', *Town and Country Planning*, May 1965.
Hugh l'Anson Fausset, *Samuel Taylor Coleridge*, Jonathan Cape, 1926.
A. G. Gardiner, *Life of George Cadbury*, Cassel, 1923.
Richard Gerber, *Utopian Fantasy: A Study of English Utopian Fiction Since the End of the Nineteenth Century*, Routledge, 1955.
Charles Gide, *Communist and Cooperative Colonies* (trans.), Harrap, 1930.
A. Gray, *The Socialist Tradition: Moses to Lenin*, Longmans, 1948.
Joyce O. Hertzler, *The History of Utopian Thought*, Macmillan, 1922.
F. R. Hiorns, *Town Building in History*, Harrap, 1956.
James Hole, *The Homes of the Working Classes with Suggestions for Their Improvement*, Longmans, 1866.
James Joll, *The Anarchists*, Eyre & Spottiswoode, 1964.
Moritz Kaufman, *Utopias, or Schemes of Social Improvement from Sir Thomas More to Karl Marx*, London, 1879.
P. Kropotkin, *Fields, Factories and Workshops*, second edition, revised and enlarged, Nelson, 1912.
Harry W. Laidler, *Social-Economic Movements*, Routledge, 1960.
Budgett Meakin, *Model Factories and Villages: Ideal Conditions of Labour and Housing*, London, 1905.
J. Reeves (Ed.), *Selected Poems of Samuel Taylor Coleridge*, Heinemann, 1959.
Thomas A. Reiner, *The Place of the Ideal Community in Urban Planning*, University of Pennsylvania Press, 1963.
Helen Rosenau, *The Ideal City in its Architectural Evolution*, Routledge, 1959.
H. Ross, *Utopias Old and New*, Nicholson & Watson, 1938.
T. S. and M. B. Simey, *Charles Booth*, Oxford University Press, 1960.

Camillo Sitte, *The Art of Building Cities*, Vienna, 1889 (trans. by Charles T. Stewart, Reinhold, New York, 1945).

J. N. Tarn, 'The Model Village at Bromborough Pool', *The Town Planning Review*, Vol. XXXV, No. 4, January 1965.

Chad Walsh, *From Utopia to Nightmare*, Geoffrey Bles, 1962.

2

Social Objectives of Town Planning

In November 1906 a deputation to the Government by the National Housing Reform Council led the Prime Minister, Sir Henry Campbell-Bannerman, to pledge that housing and town planning legislation would be introduced as soon as circumstances permitted. In the event, John Burns, President of the Local Government Board, first introduced his bill in 1908; the Housing, Town Planning etc. Act received the Royal Assent in 1909. The objectives of the legislation, to be attained by the preparation of a town planning scheme, were defined as 'proper sanitary conditions, amenity and convenience'.

These were the declared goals of planning sixty years ago. They had gained acceptance because of the weight of available evidence about the physical as well as the social conditions of the over-crowded, insanitary and rapidly developing towns of Victorian Britain. They were accepted also because the social response to a disadvantaged urban environment was seen in a very direct causal relationship. The strong belief, fed from a number of different sources, was that given the elimination of squalor from the built environment, and its proper development to give beauty and convenience, then man would emerge as a loving, happy, co-operative being, achieving a state of fulfilment. Typical had been the assumptions of James Silk Buckingham in his concept of a Model Town, Victoria, where the implications of the form of his town had moral overtones: 'From the entire absence of all wynds, courts and blind alleys, or culs-de-sac, there would be no secret and obscure haunts for the refinement of the filthy and the immoral from the public eye. . . .'[1]

These goals were accepted too because of the success of notable experiments, themselves firmly in the tradition of the century's utopian reformers, idealists, and practical exponents in the drive for better housing. Cadbury, Lever and others had established garden cities; more recently a Garden City Association had been formed for the purpose of carrying into effect Ebenezer Howard's proposals, and both private and co-operative companies commenced schemes for Garden Suburbs. The case for further action through legislation was now strong. Statistics prepared by the Garden Cities and Town Planning Association under the heading 'Life and death—the triumph of the garden city and suburbs', 'proved' the relationship with health by indicating the following rates: Hampstead Garden Suburb 4·2, Letchworth 4·8, Bournville 5·7, Port Sunlight 8·1, Bournemouth 12·35, Broomilaw 19·5, Ebbw Vale 19·7, Manchester 19·98, Liverpool 20·3, Oldham 21·46, Wigan 20·9, Shadwell 21·1, Merthyr Tydfil 21·12.[2]

Additionally of course the promise of planning legislation was secured because of the increasing recognition of the need to control the allocation of residential land and the manner in which it was laid out. Indeed, the most persuasive political pressure of the day was the rapid suburban spread of Greater London; factual evidence of growth reinforced the late Victorian horror of the big city.

The legislation of 1909 reflected the emergence of an embryo town planning movement, concerned particularly with the betterment of urban housing conditions. The new power to limit the number of houses per acre was regarded as particularly valuable. There was an obsession with 'openness' as well as the grouping of dwellings, understandably so as a reaction to the character of the development that had gone before. For example, Aldridge, secretary of the National Housing and Town Planning Council, writing in 1915 for 'councillors, officers and others engaged in the preparation of town planning schemes' indicated that 'provision shall be made in all town planning schemes not only to secure for the giving of ample space around the homes of people, but that the houses shall be well planned and well grouped, and that especially the rooms shall be so placed as to permit the sunlight to enter freely into the rooms'.[3]

But housing conditions were being improved for a purpose. The same writer declared that 'Town planning is primarily needed to increase the health and general well-being of the citizens.' The garden city reformers set out to create satisfactory communities, and this objective was at the heart of the emergent town planning movement. The wording of the title of the Act of 1909 is almost symbolic: housing and town planning went together. In other words housing and environmental improvement was not regarded as a public health exercise centred on standards for dwellings or road widths: it was a comprehensive exercise with integral social objectives.

Planning began therefore as a community-based movement, but after 1909 the events of the next decades must be seen as disappointing, leading as they did to a gradual erosion of this basic character. The reasons for this must provide an object of study in itself, but planning as a comprehensively based movement, body of thought, or discipline clearly failed to develop. This was due to a combination of factors, and it must remain a matter for conjecture at this stage which were the most important at critical times. Some of the pertinent factors (all in their turn to be seen as causes and effects) seem to have been inadequate legislation, the emergence of a professional institute which had proved to be insufficiently strong amongst the competing claims of other professional bodies, the form of local government in this country which, although with notable exceptions, has been reluctant to incorporate a strong professional planning element in its staff hierarchy, the reluctance of universities to see planning as a discipline which merited undergraduate studies, and the failure of planners themselves to develop their subject matter as an intellectual as well as a practical discipline.

Whatever the reasons, the fact has been that planning has largely betrayed its inherited traditions. Faced with continual buffeting from other professional bodies, it has always been tempted to become inward looking and fall back on residual areas of concern least disputed by other interests. For the present generation of planners this dilemma was crucial in the 1950s when a certain outlook became prevalent. The Schuster Report of 1950 indicated the lines of approach:

> . . . the function [of town planning] is to create a well balanced synthesis of what might otherwise be a mere collection of separate policies and claims, to combine them into one consistent policy for the use and development of land within the area in question, to devise the means of translating this policy in the physical conditions of that area into a plan that is practical, economic and aesthetically pleasing, and to organize the carrying through to realization of the development for which the plan has made provision.[4]

During the 1950s this line hardened. Keeble for example described town and country planning as 'the art and science of ordering the use of land and the character of siting of buildings and communication routes so as to secure the maximum practicable degree of economy, convenience and beauty'.[5] He went on to say that, 'Planning has both social and economic aims. Socially, successful Planning tends to make people's lives happier because it results in a physical environment which conduces to health, which allows convenient and safe passage from place to place, which facilitates social intercourse and which has visual attractiveness. The economic results of good Planning also, of course, conduce to increased happiness, but not quite so directly.' But to make quite clear what the planner's role was, '. . . it should be strongly emphasized that Planning . . . deals primarily with land, and is not economic, social or political Planning, though it may assist greatly in the realization of the aims of these other kinds of planning, and should obviously be made to fall in step with them'.

These extracts have been quoted, not to draw attention to the views of one particular writer, but to indicate their force as a prevalent view of the time. This interpretation of planning is at last breaking down, but only slowly, and for a large proportion of planners in professional practice the influence of old attitudes is still strong. The internal membership question of the Town Planning Institute which has arisen during the 1960s indicates however that for growing numbers a narrow and restrictive view of planning is both chafing and unrealistic.

The reasons for breaking out of the disciplinary stranglehold seem to be threefold. In the first place, it is quite impossible to overlook the origins of the town planning movement: the goals were social as well as physical and related to a total community concept. How these goals are to be achieved has to be interpreted in the light of the requirements and conditions of particular periods of time, but this is not to say that inherited goals should be jettisoned.

Secondly, the practice of planning as it has grown up in this country since the war, especially in local authority work, has shown that it is quite impossible to separate plan making from implementation, and this involves the planner in an inescapable day-to-day relationship with contributory processes carried out by the engineer, architect, surveyor, economist and sociologist. In these circumstances it is impractical to say precisely when the work of a planner begins and ends. The town planner, in order to be thoroughly effective in preparing plans, exercising his land allocating function and as a co-ordinator of activities as a plan preparer and an implementer, finds it irksome and unnecessary to be confined by traditionally conceived frontiers of particular professions or disciplines.

Thirdly, there is the question of interpretation of terms. The definition of 'environment' is notoriously difficult, but for the town planner the physical environment has been traditionally understood to be in question. This meaning must now be seen as too restrictive. The complex interrelationships within the physical, economic and social environments have become increasingly apparent and so we might now think of 'environment' in total terms: from the social point of view, it is important to recognize that an environment contains individuals, organizations and an institutional framework of social communications. An interpretation of planning simply being concerned with land is, in these circumstances, unduly confining.

This background to the views surrounding the nature of town planning, and the historical aspects of its origin, is a necessary introduction to any understanding of what 'social planning' for the town planner might be. Social planning can only be conceived in the context of a total evaluation of town planning; its objectives and role may be seen as a particular sector within that comprehensive concern. I take the view that the purpose of town planning is to promote a physical environment which is harmonious, pleasing and convenient; a related social objective is to assist in securing for man some of the means of individual personal satisfaction and happiness. This is a wide field, but the interrelated aspects of total planning practice as at present conducted fall into place: for example, determination of land use and a communications pattern to secure order and convenience; the planned provision and distribution of facilities; design to secure aesthetic qualities in the physical environment; regional planning to promote effective growth patterns in the national interest and to equalize economic opportunity, and so on. The role of social planning is the third part of the total planning trilogy, supporting the other fields of physical and economic planning.

In one sense the identification of one aspect of planning concerned with social considerations is both misleading and dangerous. First, it gives the wrong impression if it were thought that this were a self-contained part of planning, with its own techniques, approach and contribution. Second, it would create unnecessary problems if this were seen as yet another fragmentation of planning, thereby encouraging a divisive influence amongst other aspects. But on the other hand to identify social planning is, by drawing attention to a central theme of planning itself, to put new emphasis on a very neglected approach, and to give strength to a latent field of activity.

The Objectives and Roles of Social Planning

Town Planning has inherited a rich tradition, fed in the main from two sources: the social idealist and the urban designer. The mantle now worn by planners previously fell on the social reformer and the town builder. At the end of the last century housing, in the crucible of urban problems, fused the two approaches and the role of the community builder was promoted on a totally new scale.

The interpretation of the underlying objective has now to be seen in different terms. In the past, planning has been frankly paternalistic and has been developed round a philosophy of environmental determinism. There is of course undeniably *some* form of relationship between social response and the physical environment, but the extent to which this is causal must remain debatable. It is almost impossible to unravel the multiplicity of reciprocal social, physical and economic forces which fashion behaviour; it is an old adage that 'you make the environment and the environment makes you'. But the breakdown of a concept of determinism leaves no vacuum in town planning; instead it opens the gates to a liberal and much more satisfactory inter-pretation of objectives.

The basic goal remains: physical plans should serve a number of needs, and our concern here is that they should meet social requirements. The argument now is that in broad measure these social needs can only be elicited when people are able to express their desires, having first been faced with clear alternatives. Accordingly, the objective of planning is to provide these alterna-tives. The town planner's role therefore becomes permissive rather than deterministic: it is to provide a physical, social and economic framework not so much to fashion behaviour but rather to present the widest range of opportunities, and by removing constraints, to enable individuals to become 'free'. The main objective of the social aspect of planning is therefore to give satisfaction.

The opportunities for promoting satisfaction through the physical, economic and social environment are limitless. In the abstract, the physical environment may promote aesthetic satisfaction, and in the practical, the detailed arrangement or the general structure of the built environment may affect human relationships or opportunities for good or ill. The possibilities are tremendous because the influence of the environment is all-pervasive. Furthermore, the economic environment may determine job opportunities and earning power, and a whole range of social consequences stem from this. The social environment may similarly influence life-styles and general 'cultural' opportunities.

The primary social objective is therefore to open up the possibilities latent in all these aspects which have a bearing on man in society and to maximize the range of choice available for the development of individual personalities and the enrichment of social relationships. The corollary of this objective is of course to ensure that people are both better qualified and enabled to make free choices among the opportunities presented.

Such objectives relate to a broad field and confirm the inevitability of seeing town planning in very wide terms. They are applicable to all levels, whether personal, group or community, and to a variety of criteria such as education, employment and financial rewards. Freedom of choice may be a noble concept, but let there be no delusion as to how difficult it is to provide and how severe are the existing constraints operating in society. As D. R. Hunter has written in an American context:

> A man does not have a free choice if he cannot read well enough to fill out an application form or follow simple written instructions about how to perform an industrial process. He does not have free choice if he is not hired because of his color or accent. He does not have free choice if he is spiritually imprisoned by an atmosphere of hopelessness or apathy among those around him. He does not have free choice if he is an unskilled person in an economy growing too slowly and distributing its rewards in a grossly inequitable manner. He does not have free choice if he is poor.[6]

This concern with opportunity and choice has taken on a new urgency because the proliferation of technical resources encourages the widening of the gap between the 'haves' and 'have-nots'. In many ways this gap is widening, and this has political implications; the evidence from American cities at the present time is only too striking. As W. H. Auden wrote thirty years ago: 'A democracy in which each citizen is as fully conscious and capable of making a rational choice, as in the past has been possible only for the wealthier few, is the only kind of society which in the future is likely to survive for long.'[7] The contribution which planning can make in this situation therefore seems both pertinent and urgent.

In short, these social objectives of town planning are concerned with developing the potentials which life has to offer: it is a matter of revealing to people what can be done or what is available. One must stress again the revolution of thinking: the spirit of town planning does not pursue the theme of a rigidly conceived framework for personal behaviour or community structure as was envisaged in the past by such as Plato or Sir Thomas More. The question of 'dreaming of systems so perfect that no one needs to be good', in the words of T. S. Eliot,[8] forms no part of town planning. Rather, its social purpose is a medium designed to open the gate to the existence of opportunity for the greater number. As such, planning is neither deterministic, morally purposive, nor static in concept; it is adaptive, pragmatic and within broad limits permissive.

One factor immediately becomes very clear from these implications, and that is the breadth of the total planning process; the relationship between ends and means involves the town planner in a very wide field. Social objectives may be attained by a number of different measures. For example, consider the social policy of the European Coal and Steel Community.[9] This has two avowed objectives: protecting the worker and his living standards, and active promotion of projects to raise living standards and improve working conditions. The aims are to ensure continuity of income and the retraining and re-employment of workers threatened with unemployment so that workers' living standards do not bear the brunt of technological progress and economic development. Thus we see the relationship between social aspects of town planning and employment policies. In western society, joblessness is almost a form of social emasculation because of the inability to play the male role; lack or restriction of job opportunities has far-reaching social influences.

From the recognition of the social context of town planning we can proceed to draw a concept of social planning, and its objectives and role, as a specific area of concern and activity within the total process. This will take its place with other identifiable fields of interest within town planning, for example regional planning, urban design or 'statutory planning' (development control and

other matters). The goals of social planning may be briefly outlined; they are examined in greater detail in subsequent chapters.

The first aim may be stated to assist in the promotion and
furtherance of human contact. Man is a gregarious animal, and
this fact is at the heart of the nature of social life. The fundamental
social nature of man has its origin in the physiological relationship
between parent and offspring; the two are for a time bound
together in an interactive association and the life of either one or
the other is at some time dependent upon the potential or actual
being of the other. The impulses towards co-operative behaviour
are already present at birth, and all they require is cultivation.

The ethical concept of love therefore is grounded in the biological structure of man as a functioning organism; in this way, to
'love thy neighbour' in the sense of meeting the needs of others
is a social, biological as well as religious injunction. An objective
of social planning should be to allow for the interpretation of this
supportive relationship in a variety of situations. There is little
new in this theme, for the need for man's involvement with fellow
men has been a subject which has been presented constantly by a
succession of religious divines, poets, reformers, agitators and
philosophers throughout the ages. 'Any man's death diminishes
me,' declared John Donne, 'because I am involved in Mankind;
and therefore never send to know for whom the bell tolls; It
tolls for thee.'[10] Centuries later, T. S. Eliot expressed the same
concern:

> What life have you if you have not life together?
> There is no life that is not in community.[11]

Facilitating human contact promotes a vitality within society.
People are alive to the interests of others, there is support for those
in need and there is constant exposure to ranges of experiences
from a variety of backgrounds. In other words provision for human
contact promotes the development of a valuable asset in society.
In community and personal relationships there are latent forces
which may be harnessed for social benefit: for example an interest
in and tolerance towards groups of different character, an inclination towards mutual help, an ability to communicate, a drive
towards self-expression, and so on.

In short, a first objective of social planning is to assist in the
provision of both means and opportunity for the furtherance of
relationships between individuals. At a time when massive
changes are taking place especially in urban society, and when

the ties of an older social cohesion are loosening, there are indications that for certain sections of the community it is difficult to derive a rewarding and meaningful level of intimate human contact. The social planner will see his role as assisting in breaking down the constraints which operate.

At this point however he should make it clear that this policy is directed simply towards a more effective functioning of society and greater satisfaction of individuals; the policy is not conceived as an essential part of a lofty view as to the purpose of society. In explanation, we might refer as an example to Tawney, who considered that society should be organized primarily for the performance of duties and not for the maintenance of rights: '. . . if society is to be healthy, men must regard themselves not as the owners of rights, but as trustees for the discharge of functions and the instruments of a social purpose'.[12] It may be that from the point of view of personal reaction there might be a good deal of support for such an attitude; moreover, the planning objective might indeed be both relevant to and accord with Tawney's objective. But while social planning may contribute to a purposive view of society, it does not possess such a view in its own right. Social planning is a medium whereby social reformers might operate; it is not a reform movement in itself.

A second contribution of social planning concerns the needs of minorities. The widening of opportunity throughout society will largely be achieved through a universal provision which is designed to give full rein to the creativity of individuals in their search for preferences. This is effective for those in society who are adequately equipped mentally and physically to take advantage of choice, and who can throw off the restrictive constraints of the particular physical, social and economic environment to which they belong. But there are some who plainly will lack the capacity and opportunity to share in facilities provided for the total community.

There are in fact many who will be found unable to take adequate advantage of the support and amenities which society can provide—the lonely, the apathetically withdrawn, the mentally handicapped, problem families, the physically inactive, and so on. In addition there will be particular groups in society, demanding by reason of their characteristics special attention and provision. These include such as the gypsy and tinker communities, immigrants, the young, the elderly and the poor. It is in recognition of the needs of these people and many more that social work on an individual, group or community base is developed. It will be seen in the more detailed consideration of this point in later chapters that the town planner in the field of social planning has a particular contribution to make here by virtue of his techniques in survey and his co-ordinating administrative role amongst a number of disciplines or interests.

A third objective will be for the social planner to play a part in the strengthening and co-ordination of social services so that problems are tackled as efficiently and economically as possible. It will be necessary both to build up and ease the channels of communication in a community organization so that people can in fact know what choices are available, how the choice can be exercised and how they themselves can participate in activities. The aim should be to ensure that by facilitating communications those people who wish to participate in activities would find no obstacles either by way of lack of knowledge, lack of provision or the effect of underprivilege. As a corollary to this it would of course be necessary to enable those who wish to be isolated from deep community involvement to be given this opportunity.

In many neighbourhoods the community is well able to look after itself without any planned support; it may be a closely knit community where isolation is difficult or it may be an aspiring middle class community where leadership talent proliferates, so providing a large number of interconnected social groups with numerous activities. But especially in urban neighbourhoods there are many communities which patently require support and intervention to overcome the constraints which are precluding effective community organization. Social analysis will reveal those areas which present disturbing evidence of community breakdown, perhaps associated with undue concentrations of various aspects of social problems, as well as those districts which are in transition and where established patterns of social organization exclude large numbers. Here a co-ordination of three main aspects of social work will be required—the individual case worker, the group worker and the community organizer; the social planner will be able to add his own expertise and contribution.

A fourth objective in the field of social planning will be concerned with priorities. Programming is an essential part of any planning process and this should apply to any comprehensive social development plan that might be conceived. The need for priorities will constantly arise by reason of the action of pressure groups, but as money for social welfare work is always likely to be in short supply, then it is necessary to have some ideas as to the priority to be attached to various aspects.

One might suggest a number of criteria. It might be argued for example that measures to relieve poverty should be an early priority. After that there is the alternative as to whether a policy of universal provision should be favoured with a view to increasing the awareness of people to the potentials of their own environments or whether the policy should be designed to tackle the social problems of particular sections of society. It is difficult to select between the two approaches. On the one hand many people are inhibited from making the best use of their interests, talents and time, because of lack of knowledge, lack of opportunity and absence of social organization, and a relatively small amount of money per head devoted to this work might result in a substantial increase of individual satisfaction. On the other hand there are others who are much less well endowed; they have inadequate resources and an inability to utilize properly the resources they have; their needs are much greater than average. While numerically the size of some of these minority elements may be small, a much greater amount of money proportionately has to be spent in order to have a real impact.

Further work is obviously necessary to help in an evaluation of the extent to which improvements can be made in the various social fields in relation to the costs involved. At this stage it is scarcely possible to make a choice between the two approaches. It seems more likely to work on combinations of the two, and rely on the activities of pressure groups and a much more extensive social research programme to point to the greatest needs.

Conclusions

A recognition of the scope and content of town planning itself facilitates the identification of a concept of social planning. The argument expressed here is that one of the keynotes of planning is its ultimate concern with 'community' and that town planning in this country owes its existence to theoretical and literary contributions and practical experiments. But the planning movement so far has not been the best witness to its inherited traditions, and the time is very appropriate now for a rethinking of its principles and practice.

We have argued that the recognition of this new term 'social planning' is not in any way to seek to fragment, but to reinforce a comprehensive outlook. Indeed this should provide the link between the disparate elements of planning practice. In particular it will indicate the nonsense of thinking of physical planning, which has been the most widely developed aspect to date, in the contained way which has been the case so far. As Sherrard has written, 'It makes no sense to plan model cities . . . in which people will live who do not have an adequate and secure income, who do not have any real freedom or sense of dignity, no real control over their lives, and no real opportunity to assume personal, familial or communal responsibility.'[13]

The social aims of town planning have been described in terms of developing the full potential of all communities by a process of maximization of opportunity and a widening of choice. The more specific field of social planning builds on this approach, and its role and objectives have been defined as assisting in the promotion of human contact, in contributing to the strengthening and co-ordination of social services and in dealing with specific aspects of social malfunctioning or minority problems.

It is interesting to see these objectives in the light of observations from social workers themselves. Particularly relevant comments were given at the Thirteenth International Conference of Social Work in Washington in 1966 and we can usefully quote from an analysis of urban problems given by Elizabeth Wickenden. She highlighted three aspects of contemporary urban life.[14]

Firstly, there is denial of choice with respect to employment and income opportunities: 'Rarely is there enough for everyone; and many cannot, by reason of poverty or other disadvantage, reach whatever advantages the city has to offer.'

Secondly there is denial of choice with respect to the components of living by reason of urban inadequacies of provision and the pressures towards standardization and conformity.

> The exercise of choice assumes an adequate supply and a lively variety of activities, benefits, goods and services among which to choose; a practical estimate of people's needs and priorities together with a cherishing of the differences in tastes, modes of self-expression, and aptitudes that constitute the salt and savor of the human condition. But few cities in the world, even some of the richest and most beautiful approximate to this ideal. Inequalities are made glaringly visible in the slums, ghettos, shanty towns, and bidonvilles, the submarginal housing into which are crowded and isolated from the amenities of city living our poor and dispossessed.

Thirdly there is isolation of the individual from full participation in his community: '. . . neither the most far reaching social planning nor the play of market exchange, nor the interaction of the two, can afford to ignore the yearning that lies within the human spirit to express its creativity and individuality in an atmosphere of scope and variety'.

These deficiencies, for Wickenden, indicate the real areas of social need in the broadest sense. She goes on to define the sort of social environment towards which the social planner will make his own contribution.

> Man wants to live in a society which gives him not only a sense of order, security and continuity but also a sense of forward movement. He wants the security that only large-scale social organization can afford but at the same time he craves the ability to shape at least a part of his own destiny. He wants to belong to the large and massive community while retaining both his privacy and the closeness of immediate personal association. In each case he seeks to reconcile the values of a mass, urban society with his personal values, aspirations and identity.

Equally valuable comments from this Conference were given by Roger Wilson in a United Kingdom Report.[15] His conclusion was:

> What matters is that no great numbers or sections of the population should be bored or have a sense of being isolated or discriminated against, that there should be enough people from varied enough backgrounds interested in public affairs to discuss issues publicly, intelligently and appealingly, so that the public may feel themselves vicariously involved; that there should be a general atmosphere in which citizens with special interests may find it easy to form groups for pursuit of their interest—be it music, or stamp-collecting, swimming, fur and feather, darts, fishing, international affairs or knitting; and that there should be a living tradition, borne out through personal action, that sensitivity to the needs and interests of others is a good thing, even if only a limited number of people express it actively and persistently. A good community is not necessarily one which hums with universal activity. It is one in which relationships are satisfying, both vertically and horizontally, and it is towards achieving this that social policy should be directed.

In drawing up this social policy, and in the process of imple-

c

mentation, town planning has much to offer, and the time is now ripe for the role of the social planner to be developed.

REFERENCES TO CHAPTER 2

1. James Silk Buckingham, *National Evils and Practical Remedies*, London, 1849.
2. Henry R. Aldridge, *The Case for Town Planning*, National Housing and Town Planning Council, 1915.
3. Henry R. Aldridge, *op. cit.*
4. The Schuster Report, *Report of the Committee on the Qualifications of Planners*, Cmd. 8509, H.M.S.O., 1950.
5. Lewis Keeble, 'Principles and Practice of Town and Country Planning', *Estates Gazette*, 1952.
6. David R. Hunter, *The Slums—Challenge and Response*, The Free Press of Glencoe, 1964.
7. Barbara Everett, *Auden*, Oliver & Boyd, 1964.
8. T. S. Eliot, *Choruses From 'The Rock'*, Collected Poems, 1909–35, Faber & Faber, 1949.
9. 'Social Policy in the European Coal and Steel Community, 1953–65', *Community Topics* No. 20, European Community Information Service, 1966.
10. John Donne, *Devotions*, xvii, 1624, Nonesuch Edition, editor John Hayward, Random House, New York, 1928.
11. T. S. Eliot, *op. cit.*
12. R. H. Tawney, *The Acquisitive Society*, Bell, 1921.
13. Thomas D. Sherrard, *Social Welfare and Urban Problems*, Columbia University Press, 1968.
14. Elizabeth Wickenden, 'What are the Social Priorities for the Modern City and How do we Achieve Them?', in *Urban Development—its Implications for Social Welfare*, Proceedings of the XIIIth International Conference of Social Work, Washington D.C., September 1966, Columbia University Press, 1967.
15. Roger Wilson, 'Social Aspects of Urban Development', editor G. M. Lomas, in the United Kingdom Report on *Social Welfare Implications of Urban Development*, prepared for the XIIIth International Conference of Social Work, Washington, 1966.

3

Social Issues for the Town Planner

We have shown in the previous chapter that a distinct area of concern, social planning, might be identified within the parent field of town planning itself. The context of town planning has a social base, and while the 'social planner' will develop a specialist role, there is a range of social issues relevant to planning as a whole. In this chapter we look in a general way at some of these issues in which the town planner should be conversant at the present time. The specialist social planner will take these up in greater detail as matters of study, to assist in planning policy making and, in a wider role, to contribute to the implementation of policy.

There is increasing awareness that the most important contemporary planning issues, and particularly research interests, lie not within the province of traditionally conceived disciplines but on the overlapping borders between them. This is particularly true in the social sciences where planners have to a large extent always been dependent on other disciplines for their insight into the nature of towns and regions or the functioning of communities; geographers, economists and sociologists have all played their part. There has been a new focussing of interest and a significant expansion of interdisciplinary research work in recent years in the general context of urban studies, with the result that planners are increasingly challenged to be familiar with a widening range of new findings. It is not an easy task to attempt to keep up to date with analyses of rapidly changing physical, social and economic questions in urban and rural environments, for which planning policies have to be formulated.

The town planner clearly requires a thorough grounding in social studies relating to both town and country. Without this, social planning objectives will always tend to be poorly conceived, and policies will rely on emotional lobby rather than objective formulation. At the best, the social aspects of planning will rest on outmoded principles, out of tune with changed circumstances. The 'neighbourhood', 'balanced communities' and 'community feeling' are already some of the terms freely used in planning with neither precision nor real understanding, overt or implied.

There is a tradition of social planning, but as a modern concept it is scarcely formulated, and in practice there are limited achievements; indeed, there is so much confusion that it is difficult to explain what are the social bases of planning today. Perhaps it is that there is no policy framework, merely an *ad hoc* collection of rough rules of thumb laced with imperfectly understood sociological jargon, and resting on a philosophical base developed in the last century. More likely, the hard pressed planner might express his *credo* in terms of provision of new housing and all that implies in terms of living standards, the creation of new communities with planned facilities and new opportunities, and the fostering of neighbourliness. In fact much of the work under the name of social planning has been undertaken in New Towns, where at least there are Social Development Officers, but elsewhere local planning authorities usually have a very truncated view of the integration of social policies with physical planning objectives.

In the light of the arguments outlined in the last chapter, a very substantial shift of emphasis is required conceptually within the planning profession, and within the local planning authorities as practitioners, if planning is to express its full philosophy. There has been a marked reluctance to recognize that planning has any wider role at all other than in the purely physical field (although from the regional point of view economic planning is clearly in the ascendancy). But the time is now ripe for planning to come of age, and in full maturity to develop its social philosophy and to reveal itself as a creative process in full harmony and integration with other social objectives.

For it to do so, planners need to reveal a far greater awareness of interrelationships in the physical, social and economic environment. The connection between good housing and community satisfaction has long been recognized, if sometimes overstated; this has been the case during virtually the whole of the last century. Indeed almost 100 years ago Octavia Hill was to write firmly, 'You cannot deal with people and their houses separately.'[1] But surprisingly little interest by and large has been shown by planners in developing ecological research in this direction. All too often planners have been insufficiently demanding in questioning facts, old attitudes and policies, being markedly content to accept a crude environmental determinism that the reduction, if not eradication, of social problems might be achieved through new housing and integrative neighbourhood projects.

The full recognition of the social context of town planning, and the emergence of social planning, both in concept and practice as a specialist field, has been hindered by two main obstacles. The first is the inherent nature of planning itself, namely the dilemma as to whether a static or an adaptive outlook is to be the basic approach. The second, stemming from the first, has been the obsession with finite physical sciences, rather than the social sciences, and hence the reluctance to recognize society, in all its changing aspects, as a proper and necessary basis of planning study. It is useful to look at these two points in greater detail.

The question of change in the environment is crucial and there are real doubts as to whether the traditional outlook of planning is any longer adequate to encompass this in its field. Conceptually, town planning may be regarded as either static or adaptive. A static approach implies fixed goals over time, and in consequence the requirement of a disciplined planning administrative machine to achieve these goals. On the other hand, an adaptive approach to planning implies flexibility in goal setting and a reliance on the continual revision of broad guidelines to monitor long-term goals. This in turn suggests that the nature of the planning machine should attach greater importance to an analytical content and a multi-disciplinary approach to a study of total environment and its constant patterns of change than is at present the case.

The static view of planning has, as its tradition, a basis of plan-making specialists, and in post-war years has been emphasized by development plans as a key feature of planning machinery. It has resulted in the planning profession being characterized by those concerned with the preparation of two- and sometimes three-dimensional schemes of development as finite, fixed goals of intent. From the commissioned plan, which was a feature of the interwar period and the early and mid-1940s, this outlook fell easily into the post-1947 period. The importance of this is twofold: firstly it emphasized planning as being concerned with the consolidation of fixed goals, and secondly it necessitated a large section of its professional members being concerned with day-to-day processes designed to safeguard the sanctity of those goals. In other words the establishment of planning as a bureaucratic arm of government (local and central) has had the result of imparting a distinct flavour to the character of planning itself, both conceptually and from the point of view of its process. This concentration has left insufficient energy or time to develop adequately that side of planning which is more concerned with the understanding of physical, social and economic forces which affect a given situation or which might affect a particular scheme which has been prepared.

It is easy to exaggerate, but still very necessary to recognize, this dichotomy of outlook within planning. It is certainly one which is not bridged by a requirement for five-yearly reviews of development plans or the constant, but usually fairly shallow, reappraisal of policies whch is always ongoing. The full recognition of an adaptive approach to planning allows for a rather different type of goal setting. The definition of 'adaptive' in this sense is 'being modified to conditions' and to that extent planning goals are looser, less rigid in both time and content, being guidelines rather than a fixed physical frame. Moreover, the related planning process is weighted towards analysis and a deeper understanding of situations, trends and issues, and a necessarily broader, interdisciplinary approach to problems. This planning work is quite different from that which is responsive to a fixed physical frame.

Static and adaptive types of planning are of course to be found side by side in the same planning team or organization, but it is true to say that as far as local planning authorities are concerned (and these reflect the principal image of planning work in this country) the main characteristic is an addiction to the static approach. Once established, this tends to be self-reinforcing and the time has surely been reached when an important reversal of attitudes is necessary. Certain local planning authorities prove the exception to the rule and have played a valuable part in contributing to and feeding an adaptive approach; here research and survey teams have kept alive the spirit of questioning accepted views, and of course the strength of the total planning team has benefited considerably. But by and large it is fair to recognize that planning has become well and truly immersed in a static outlook, conceptually and in terms of process.

The key to the approach to static or adaptive planning lies in attitudes towards the nature of the physical and social environment. An adaptive approach recognizes the dynamic element and it is precisely this which in the past planning has found difficult to grasp. As Jane Jacobs writes: '. . . while city planning has [thus] mired itself in deep misunderstanding about the very nature of the problem with which it is dealing, the life sciences, unburdened with this mistake, and moving ahead very rapidly, have been providing some of the concepts that city planning needs: along with providing the basic strategy of recognizing problems of organized complexity, they have provided hints about analysing and handling this kind of problem'.[2]

This examination of the fundamentals of planning is of course not only of relevance to the social planner, but to all connected with planning and its process, because at the centre of the problem lies a new concept of the nature of planning and its area of concern. So far, as we said, the approach to planning has been to regard the town, city or larger community as having purely a spatial, physical form. Plans have accordingly been conceived as static distributions of land uses or activities. But there is now the contrary view that we should see the city or city region not in these terms at all but as 'a complex interaction of diverse and functionally interdependent parts, with the parts evolving over time as they seek to adapt to the ever changing contexts around them'.[3] The city in this way is a social system in action, and this replaces the traditional view of the city conceived as an artifact with a land-use pattern. Such a concept brings the social planner into the very heart of planning; his contribution is not merely a subsequent activity once a spatial system has been conceived.

Webber takes the argument further. Speaking in respect of the American situation, he views the long-term prospect for urbaniza-tion as a maze of sub-cultures within a very diverse society organ-ized on a broadly shared cultural base. He contends that 'the essential qualities of urbanness are cultural in character, not terri-torial, that these qualities are not necessarily tied to the conceptions that see the city as a spatial phenomenon'.[4]

Planning thought of in this way is therefore clearly concerned with the social, political and economic organization of the com-munity and its constituent parts. This is in fact the basis of an adaptive approach to planning, a quite different base from that of a static concept. Up till now planning has been obsessed with the idea of place; instead, it is argued that the essence of the city and city life is interaction. Urban communities are not merely places but processual systems in which people interact with each other. This assumption gives planning a radically different starting point from previous concepts, and involves the practising planner in a much more fundamental concern for community studies than has so far been recognized.

This examination of fundamental issues has taken us an important step forward. We have discussed earlier how the planning movement emerged from a series of circumstances and events, particularly of the nineteenth century, and central to its ideals was concern for society. In this, planning shares in an important ground swell of humanitarian regard for better living conditions and the search for new social systems. In the twentieth century, planning has struggled without great success to embody its social ideal within a largely physical planning system. The time is now right for a reappraisal of both concept and practice, and we are helped to this end by reverting to seeing the 'community' not as the end product of planning but as the starting point. Only a slight readjustment of outlook is necessary: instead of an idealistic concern for society, perhaps implying *a priori*, moralistic judgements as to how people should behave or how a community should be structured, we should adopt a factual concern for society, implying the need to understand fully the forces of changes within a community make-up and within the interrelated context of a given spatial system.

Having taken this intellectual hurdle, a whole new area is opened up for the town planner in the social field. He is no longer obliged to stand on traditionally conceived, disciplinary sidelines. He has both to become familiar with, and contribute to, a new wide area of social studies if the comprehensive policies which he is asked to frame are to be formulated in adequate recognition of the complex issues of changing environments. Current social issues for the town planner are many and varied, but we might attempt a summary as follows. In the first place he should be thoroughly cognizant of recent community studies and their relevant conclusions, which have been produced in some quantity in recent years.

Then there are a number of aspects which the specialist social planner should consider in some depth. First, there are changes in the structure of society, such as the impact of urbanism or industrialism; also changing social class differences, and the changing character of social life in communities and neighbourhoods. Secondly, there is the need for greater awareness of forces (physical, social and economic) which are affecting the process of change, both decay and growth, of and within towns. Residential areas for example change in character and there are a whole set of social causes and consequences which merit further study.

Thirdly, he should be aware of the issues concerning population movement: the continuing process of spatial redistribution and the forces, both cause and effect, which attend it. There is the question for example of social forces in housing demand and the social issues surrounding housing redevelopment. Fourthly, there is the large field of 'environment and behaviour': the phenomenon of urban decay and social disorganization, and their relationship.

So far the issues described have been urban ones. But there are rural problems too and the planner has to be familiar with changing rural characteristics. The question of depopulation has long been recognized but there are also problems surrounding the changing nature of rural settlements and economy. How far is it possible indeed to speak now of truly rural areas at all?

Lastly, there is the issue of leisure in mass society. This is really a subject in its own right, but it can properly be mentioned in this context. With wider affluence, greater free time and the stimulus of higher education, new social forces demand the provision of recreational facilities on an unprecedented scale.

As we have remarked, these social issues in town planning are characterized by change, and it is in the analysis and understanding of changing social factors in the environment that planning has been almost at its weakest. There is really no reason why this should continue to be so, and we need go no further at the outset than refer to the large number of community studies published in recent years. These have produced a considerable amount of accessible material and the town planner should obviously be conversant with them.

British community studies have largely followed those in America by investigating interrelations between sets of institutions in a particular locality. The tradition was set by the Lynds's study of *Middletown* and later *Middletown in Transition;* Herbert Gans's *Levittowners* continues the pattern. In Britain Margaret Stacey's study of Banbury, *Tradition and Change,* follows this tradition, but elsewhere there have been concentrations on certain institutions to the relative exclusion of others. *Coal is our Life* was the study of a Yorkshire mining community with a focus on workplace. *Small Town Politics,* a study of Glossop, was concerned with political institutions. *The Sociology of an English Village* on the other hand dealt with the question of land in Gosforth (Cumberland) and an interrelationship with family and class. Yet again

The Family and Social Change studied the institution of the family in Swansea.

Perhaps the most well-known study for British planners has been that of Willmott and Young, *Family and Kinship in East London*. This built up a picture of working class life in Bethnal Green, comparing it with a different residential situation in the wider metropolitan area, 'Greenleigh'. A number of complementary studies such as that by Hilda Jennings in respect of Bristol, and by Vereker and Mays describing the Crown Street area of Liverpool, also made their emotional impact in planning quarters because of their concern with the break-up of communities in redevelopment areas, always a volatile area of public comment.

These studies have contributed to our understanding of contemporary British society and it is clearly incumbent upon the planner to read widely in this field. Local communities often have highly individual characteristics, and reliance on highly generalized ideas about matters such as 'kinship', the 'family' or 'class system' can be frankly dangerous for micro-planning where a real understanding of local situations is demanded if the framing of policies and techniques of execution are to be competently handled. Many residential redevelopment schemes have been badly managed because the character and functioning of the community concerned had been imperfectly understood.

Local communities change, some slowly and some rapidly, but local populations are rarely static for long either in composition or character. This demands the faithful monitoring and feedback of the characteristics of all local communities. The planner has been helped tremendously in recent years not only by community studies as outlined above, but also by the availability of comprehensive socio-economic data for small areas (Enumeration Districts). The tool of social area analysis is a valuable one for assessing critical changes over periods of time, and when followed by other research methods such as participant observation and other forms of surveys, this enables the planner to understand more fully the social base of his work and the continual ongoing process of change.

Changes in Society

We can now consider some of the aspects with which the specialist social planner may wish to be concerned in some detail. Of these,

structural changes in society and changes in the internal functioning of communities are fundamental. These changes have been
marked during this century, and in many ways may be thought to
be accelerating in pace. There are a number of issues here and
space only permits passing reference, but it will be useful to point
to at least three important areas of concern. One is the effect of
urbanism on our way of life, with its massive impact on society.
Another is the question of changing social class differences, so
important in the British context. Yet another is neighbourhood
or residential area change, which gives rise to important local
characteristics.

Urbanism

Possibly the most important feature of recent decades to affect the
total planning situation has been the quite remarkable growth of
sizes of towns, both absolutely and relatively to total population.
The etymological kinship between 'cities' and 'civilization' has
been emphasized in the twentieth century: contemporary civilization is city-based.

The situation for the planner is simply that much of world
society is now urban. This is not to say that rural communities do
not exist, but merely to recognize a basic characteristic. The number of cities in the world with a population of 100,000 and over
increased from 36 in 1800 to 678 in 1930 and 1,128 in 1960, the
accumulated totals of population of these cities rising from 11·5
millions to 243 millions to 590 millions in the same years.[5]

In Britain the critical change was to be seen in the nineteenth
century with a complete restructuring of the urban–rural relationship. By 1851 the urban population of Britain had just overtaken
the rural, and by 1881 the urban figure was more than double the
rural. The twentieth century has seen the continuing erosion of
the rural sector of the population—not only numerically but also
from the point of view of what might be thought to constitute a
specifically rural way of life. Mass media of communications have
severely diffused the distinction between rural and urban criteria.

This pace of urbanization has had widespread social consequences. For example there is the question of being uprooted from
a rural agricultural community or small town when a sense of community, identification or continuity may be severed. In contrast,
the new urban environment may be anonymous and uncertain.
Then there is the impact perhaps of a new form of employment,
which, if it is repetitive in a specialized function, creates problems

of finding creative satisfaction. Underlying this there is the impact of new ideas, new concepts and new values which few can withstand with ease.

It is now thirty years since Louis Wirth drew attention to the consequences of urbanism. He argued that as a social order urbanism was characterized by the substitution of secondary for primary, personal contacts. The key features were the weakening of kinship ties, the declining significance of the local neighbourhood, the undermining of the traditional bases of social solidarity and the transfer of industrial, educational and recreational activities to specialized institutions.

One result of the internal structure of cities was compartmentalization.

Diverse population elements inhabiting a compact settlement [thus] tend to become segregated from one another in the degree in which their requirements and modes of life are incompatible with one another and in the measure in which they are antagonistic to one another. Similarly persons of homogeneous status and needs unwittingly drift into, consciously select, or are forced by circumstances into the same area. The different parts of the city thus acquire specialized functions. The city consequently tends to resemble a mosaic of social worlds in which the transition from one to the other is abrupt.[6]

This is an observation which is helpful in recognizing the forces behind the internal structuring of cities. This is not the time to question the process as understood by Wirth, although certainly modifications to his thesis have been required. The point is merely made that town planners should be familiar with the massive changes which have taken place, together with their causes and consequences.

With regard to the character of an urban way of life, Wirth argued that man thinks, feels and responds differently in the city than outside it, and that the growth of a city is accompanied by a substitution of indirect secondary relations for direct primary relations. Man in fact has been transformed by long city life. Superficiality, anonymity and the transitory character of urban social relations had led to sophistication and a new rationality. Money economy had led to a matter-of-fact attitude in dealing with men and things. On the credit side, in city life the individual gains a certain degree of emancipation from personal and emotional controls of intimate groups, but on the other hand there is a loss of spontaneous self-expression and sense of participation that comes from living in an integrated society.

Recognition of the new urban society which is so profoundly different from previous societies is of great importance. Wirth considered the city a complex of human beings exhibiting the most extraordinary heterogeneity, a feature which was a source not only of ferment and stimulation but also frictions and conflicts. He saw urban life characterized by the presence of close physical proximity coupled with vast social difference of men. A new form of social organization was emerging in which, instead of kinship and tradition, interest and ideology cemented human individuals into effective working groups. The basis of human association had altered and simpler social organizations were subjected to severe strains.

Wirth was writing a generation ago, and this interpretation of changes in urban society was associated with some gloomy forebodings. Perhaps it had its effect in certain quarters by stimulating interest in 'community' via the neighbourhood and this was certainly a forceful lobby during the 1940s. But no sooner have planners during the last generation become accustomed to Wirth's generalizations than important refinements to the general thesis are now being offered.

We recall that 'urban impersonality' was a characteristic stressed by Wirth; but perhaps we should say rather more about this now. A study of the Piedmont Industrial Crescent of North and South Carolina, containing the towns of Raleigh, Durham, Burlington, Greenboro, High Point, Winston–Salem and Charlotte, has recently looked at this question of individuals' personal relationships. The authors found that the lives of people of two of the cities (Durham and Greenboro, admittedly of small size) were certainly enveloped in an impersonal atmosphere, but maintain that impersonality is not a central characteristic, but much more an added dimension of social participation.[7]

Their findings were that seven out of every ten men, and three out of every ten women, have impersonal contacts every day. Eighty per cent of the men and half the women have such contacts very frequently if not daily. Three-quarters of the men and almost as many women apparently enjoy such contacts and only seven per cent of the sample definitely disliked them. But to the authors this does not mean that the inhabitants of Durham and Greenboro are deprived of close, affectional social ties. For the most part, their marriages are satisfactory, and they have a sufficient number of satisfactory relationships with friends and kinsmen. In general, they have made a satisfactory adjustment to the relatively superficial urban neighbourhood social patterns and to the necessity of dealing impersonally with a large number of people.

The 'urban way of life' has not prevented most individuals from achieving a reasonably contented existence. Kinsmen and friends continue to play an important part in the lives of people, even though they may not live in the same neighbourhood. This evidence from North and South Carolina is important and relevant to current thinking about living in towns in Britain. It was fashionable at one time to talk about the barrenness of suburban estates in terms of personal contacts and to eulogize the contrasting friendliness of the slums. There is a large amount of personal contact in all types of residential areas, and the presumed increasing amount of impersonal contact does not seem to be giving rise to an urban population miserably lost in anonymity.

Wirth's view on the urban way of life therefore now needs some redefinition. Generalizations will not suffice, and only the constant monitoring both of the changing characteristics of urban communities and satisfactions derived from different physical and social environments, will give the planner adequate guidance for his policy making.

An issue closely related to urbanism is the impact of industrialism on society. There have been social changes in the last century by reason of the effect of industrialization just as much as urbanization; indeed, the consequences of the two have gone hand in hand. The Industrial Revolution transformed the social structure of medieval society, and the nineteenth century saw the accelerated destruction of a land-based aristocracy and guild-based monopolies. A greater division of labour and more social divisions were created than ever before. To put these events into context, industrialism might be seen as one of four sequent stages in recent urban dvelopment: urban growth, industrialism, the emergence of a middle class and the rise of nationalism as the unifying political ideology. Reissman has argued that these features have characterized the nineteenth-century city in the West.[8]

But it is during the twentieth century that the massive social changes associated with industrialism have been effected, with results in, for example, education, class structure, political forms and dominant social values. A new way of life has been forged with new standards set for work, leisure, motivations and aspirations. Industrialism has helped to blur the division between city and country and, as we have seen, urban ideas and urban values have spread out increasingly to dominate the whole of society.

Another linked aspect of social change concerns the family. The basic issue here is that the effects of industrialization and urbanization have reinforced the tendencies towards the miniaturization of the family and the loosening of the bonds within it. The change has been marked in the last century. From an American point of view, Frankel has written graphically, 'Even a hundred years ago the grandmother who knew her place was a matriarch. Now, if she is lucky and moves as though she were treading on eggshells, she may just qualify as a friend.'[9]

For the planner there are a number of issues stemming from this situation. In the first place for example the social cohesion which existed with strong family networks, and which marked old neighbourhoods, has been disrupted, and this has been emphasized with enforced redevelopment and rehousing. Attempts have been made to allow for these forces of disruption, though with little success, but the matter does not stop there, for now there is a new factor to consider. Rosser and Harris in their study of Swansea have suggested that the dispersed kinship grouping, although wider than the elementary family, has the same composition as the classical extended family.[10]

Secondly, the fragmentation of the family has had an important effect on household formation rates and the necessity to provide dwellings of a particular size for the elderly. Where retired people have migrated, for example in Britain to south coast resorts, a new problem has emerged, not only for the elderly themselves but also for the local authorities which have accommodated them in such numbers.

These then briefly are some of the factors surrounding the question of social change related to the impact of urbanism. We have referred here to underlying 'structural' forces, but there are in addition of course demographic factors such as changing birth and death rates, the age pyramid, marriage rates, and so on; these however are of somewhat different character from the issues on which we have focussed attention.

Social Class Patterns of Behaviour

Another social issue which is of relevance for the planner's understanding of change in the community is that of differences in life styles between social classes and the degree to which shifts are taking place between recognizable class divisions. Norms of personal or group behaviour are readily identifiable features in a social environment. They reflect social expectancies and aspirations and as such constitute important social forces in seeking, for example, housing and environmental satisfaction. These forces are constantly assuming new facets, and planners should recognize the factors involved.

So far, the planner has paid only a passing interest to this field. Once again he has tended to fall victim to a reliance on environmental determinism. Until recently, the dislocation of an existing community with its particular social system or behavioural patterns by reason of slum clearance has not caused the professional alarm which it should have done. The planner has been inclined to be apathetic to the consequences and rely on the sociologist to 'tell him what to do'. The planner has had confidence in the fact that new residential areas are being provided and the belief that a benign influence will be bestowed to produce a benevolent and conforming local culture. Instead, as a first step, he should be obliged to be familiar with the social characteristics of the community for which he is making plans, just as much as he is expected to gain working knowledge of physical criteria, whether they are traffic flows or microclimate.

Changes in life styles over time have been well documented. The remarks of an amateur, but perceptive, observer, James Kirkup of the North-East might be quoted. Kirkup, a native of South Shields, tells of his childhood there in the 1920s and '30s.[11] In his memories of personal events he provides a real insight into the cultural heritage of Tyneside—'aal tigither like the foaks o'Shiels'. He describes his native Cockburn Street, returning to his home town after ten years' absence:

The streets had an air of prosperity, solidity and quiet ease, far different from the miasma of grim poverty and despair in the twenties, when we used to go running along behind the galloping coal-carts in the hope that a lump of coal might be shaken off. . . .

I walked slowly back along the street. Two women were talking in front of one of the corner shops, but there was none of that vital communal commotion which I remembered from my early days, when on a fine evening like this every family would be chatting on its front doorstep and the street would be full of skipping and chanting children. The life of the little community seemed to be shut away behind closed doors or sucked into the blank milky-blue screens of the telly's sacred shrine that occasionally glimmered eerily through a curtained window.

There have been differences over time; the nature of social life has changed, in the case of the working class community in South Shields due to both local circumstances and massive changes in emphasis which have affected society in general. But there are also differences between communities and their behaviour patterns at any given period of time. For example there is the traditional working class urban home described by Richard Hoggart:

> It is a cluttered and congested setting, a burrow deeply away from the outside world. There is no telephone to ring, and knocks at the door in the evening are rare. But the group, though restricted, is not private: it is a gregarious group in which most things are shared, including personality; 'our Mam', 'our Dad', 'our Alice' are normal forms of address. To be alone, to think alone, to read quietly is difficult. There is the wireless or television, things being done in odd bouts, or intermittent snatches of talk (but rarely a sustained conversation); the iron thumps on the table, the dog scratches and yawns or the cat miaows to be let out; the son drying himself on the family towel near the fire whistles, or rustles the communal letter from his brother in the army which has been lying on the mantelpiece behind the photo of his sister's wedding; the little girl bursts into a whine because she is too tired to be up at all, the budgerigar twitters.[12]

This might be contrasted with an elegant, middle class home, Crestwood Heights in Canada.

> The Crestwood home must ideally provide ample space for separate sleeping and working quarters for each member of the family. There should be a desk or its equivalent in a well-demarcated area for each member of the family 'old-enough'. These areas may be rooms or merely corners, shelves or drawers within a larger room; and little pressure is put on the individual to keep this area tidy. When occupying 'his space', the individual should not be disturbed; when absent, his possessions are not to be rearranged. A place for the mother may be the entire kitchen with a still more private corner where she keeps household bills, personal correspondence, recipes, receipts, and money; the boy may have a lab, or a darkroom, and a place for skates, skis, and other gear; the father will have a spot to keep his tobacco pipes, golf clubs, bridge set, and he may possibly also have a workshop; the

girl, similarly, will screen cherished items—letters, photos, diary, cosmetics—from the eyes of other family members. The bedroom is often the repository of most of these items of personal property around which the individual builds his own satisfactions and which help to differentiate him from the other members of the inner circle of his life; indeed he will often reveal them more freely to a peer in age and sex than to a member of his own family. If he leaves home he will take these possessions with him.[13]

The planner finds much of interest in the recognition of social patterns, and we have argued that an adaptive approach to planning depends on accurate evaluations of the characteristics of existing communities and the continual process of change which is affecting them. Planning so far has made a poor showing in this respect. Consider for example where a sub-culture might be thought to exist in socal problem areas: by and large, planning has quite failed to understand the problems of these and there has been a total inability to match the objectives of social planning with achievements in physical planning.

Most large cities have their 'sumps' as social problem areas and it is unlikely that urban renewal will achieve very much overall improvement in the circumstances of the people while ever the effect is to discipline or scatter these communities, an end result which is all too common. A consequence is to drive the under-privileged of these communities further into retreat because all the planner has been able to do in the past is to appeal to the dominant middle class values of society, believing that conforming norms of behaviour will emerge from the eradication of poor housing conditions. It is all right for the Levittowns of this world: here the planner provides opportunities that reflect people's aspirations: 'Perhaps more than any other type of community, Levittown permits most of its residents to be what they want to be—to centre their lives around the home and the family, to be among neighbours whom they can trust, to find friends to share leisure hours, and to participate in organizations that provide sociability and the opportunity to be of service to others.'[14]

But planning policies have to be framed for communities very different from Levittown: one for example which may be apathetic, intolerant, frightened or quasi-criminal, a community which may not be neighbourly and may lack an integrating organization, being held together more by hostility to the outside world. The traditional appeal to middle class values here will simply fail; moreover new behavioural norms will not necessarily emerge from new housing conditions.

Pertinent background material for the planner in the field of social change is also to be seen in those movements which may occur from working class to middle class affiliations. In spite of an expectancy to the contrary, surveys have suggested that the increasing affluence of the bulk of the population is not necessarily leading to the assumption of middle class standards by the working class. Similarly, a change of housing and environmental conditions from an old neighbourhood to a new estate is not accompanied by a rejection of inherited ways of life.

Class differentials are being stubbornly maintained, and we might refer to Goldthorpe's work testing the thesis of 'embourgeoisement'.[15] Basing his study on a sample of industrial workers at Luton, he was interested in finding how rising living standards among the industrial labour force might have political consequences in switching allegiances from Labour to Conservative parties. We need not dwell on this particular issue, but his general findings are of relevance for the planner.

The Luton survey gave little indication that the affluent workers studied were in process of being assimilated into middle class society; 'middle classness' was not simply a matter of money. The position of a group within a system of social stratification was not decisively determined by the income or possessions of its members, but rather by their characteristic life-chances and experiences and by the nature of their relationships with other groups. The affluent workers of Luton have been brought within reach of a middle class standard of income and consumption, but only through a kind of work which is not typically part of white-collar experience. 'Getting ahead' for manual wage workers cannot be the same as in the middle class sense; rather, it rests in the progressive increase of the rewards gained from their present economic role.

Consequently, the survey suggested that important differences are maintained between the middle class and the affluent workers. For example, the latter tend towards the traditional working class belief that the home is a place reserved for kin and for certain friends—quite different from a middle class characteristic of social life that couples entertain each other in their own homes. In this way a distinction is preserved between a residential area characterized by a home-centred social base and one where the feature is one of reliance much more on external social meeting places such as the club or pub. This has its practical planning significance in the planned distribution of social facilities for different communities.

Local Communities

Concern with social mobility focusses attention on movements of people from one social class to another. But this sort of mobility is almost invariably associated with geographical movement from one community, one neighbourhood or one social circle to another. This is important for anyone concerned with the planning of communities, if only because these migrants appear at first in the role of newcomers and perhaps as outsiders to an already established set of people.

This was the theme of a study of a small community in Leicestershire with a relatively old settlement as its core and two more recent settlements which have formed around it.[16] The image which the old neighbourhoods had of the newer one persisted: the newer neighbourhood where delinquency was thought rampant was stigmatized, and this opinion persisted even though the facts of the situation changed.

But of wider importance facing the planner are the practical issues concerning the changing character of local communities at the neighbourhood level. For example old districts in twilight areas may change dramatically when under certain conditions they may be rejected by an existing population and sought out by a new one—a different ethnic group, a different social class and occupational group, or perhaps a different age group. This process of social change has been recorded in a number of cities. Typical here is the Victorian suburb, formerly prosperous and well-to-do, sought out during a particular period for occupancy of a different social character, in most cases the artisan and the less well-to-do. Under particular conditions the cycle may continue with a renewed occupancy by the middle class.

Less dramatic, and not as well recorded are the changes which take place within new housing estates. One example was the Berinsfield study by Morris and Mogey which, using repeated interviews and an adequate control group, looked at the development of social relations on a new estate.[17] The 'phase hypothesis' tested here was that firstly, for the first three to six months of an estate's life exploration and openness are the main features of social relationships in order to overcome common problems. Following this, when the estate grows to a size when it is no longer possible to know everyone, the influx of new neighbours threatens the intimacy which was developing and the small group structure disintegrates. Lastly, when the social structure becomes settled and friendships and cliques are established, an equilibrium is reached between the first and second phase.

Within the context of this general theme the Berinsfield study emphasized the importance of small residential groups containing ten to fifteen adult members which act as primary groups encompassing the family. They establish standards for furnishing and for judging the prestige of the home and residential area. By comparison the large residential group is less clearly defined, with only little family structure and it may function irregularly. The planner should find immediate significance in this as he attempts to make provision for a meaningful social organization within a neighbourhood. Cohesion focussed on child play groups or the small environmental area would seem to be suggested.

An appreciation of the ever-changing function and social role of the British neighbourhood and the character of social life within may also be helped to some extent by comparisons with America. A helpful source in this respect is Bracey's study of neighbours on new estates and sub-divisions in England and the U.S.A.[18] The inquiry studied the adjustment of urban families to life in new rural–urban fringe neighbourhoods, first of all near Bristol and subsequently near Columbus, Ohio.

It is helpful to refer to one or two of the conclusions. The American sub-divisions showed much greater neighbourliness than English estates. In the choice of a new neighbourhood both groups of nationals rated highly its accessibility relative to the husband's place of work. On the other hand the Americans sought a good school system but the English did not. Yet again, the English sought nearness of open country, but the Americans did not.

Many women on English estates experienced loneliness but this was not the case on American sub-divisions. In English neighbourhoods there were complaints of too few organizations for adults and especially children. No English organization, religious or secular, appeared to be adequately equipped to welcome newcomers or to recruit them to their membership. On the other hand, in both countries children were important in bringing adults together for neighbourly intercourse. In America increased neighbourliness is reflected by the open layout and the invitations to informal coffee sessions. In England, where more frequently only carefully chosen guests are invited in, the dimensions of sitting rooms are based on purely family use. In America on the other hand, the modern home is planned to accommodate parties of up to thirty guests and kitchens are designed to provide refreshments for these numbers at great speed. We have argued that the planner should be concerned with aspects of social change. The comparison of British and American experience is significant if there is a belief that the British situation in the future will tend to resemble that of America today.

Changes in Urban Structure

The constant process of change in urban structure is a feature most marked in larger towns and cities with an important element of nineteenth-century housing where the twin forces of urban growth and decay are now both in evidence. The former is linked most obviously with questions concerning population movement and housing demand and this is taken up in a later section. Here, as an example of the issues involved we shall refer to the process of urban decay and accompanying social changes, now characterizing the twilight zones of inner neighbourhoods.

This is a tremendously important question at the present time when housing and planning policies generally are being formulated to tackle a wide variety of social, economic and physical problems. Since the war renewal investment has been concentrated in areas of unfit housing with the aim of clearing slums and achieving redevelopment. With the exception of real blackspots in the country, notably Clydeside and parts of the North-West, the main problem has now shifted from unfitness to inadequacy of dwellings and thereby from clearance to rehabilitation. Large inner areas of our larger towns are now earmarked for this new planning interest, and it is most important for planners to be thoroughly acquainted with the character and function of residential areas they are to retain and reshape. This is a field of work where the specialist social planner should be central to the total planning process in the attempt to marry social objectives and physical requirements in renewal. At the present time it may be fairly said that we know too little about the processes of urban decay and the underlying social, economic and physical issues. Additionally, we lack knowledge about the function and characteristics of twilight areas.

In many ways this is surprising, and clearly a substantial research field is relatively unexplored. Changes in the internal structure of cities over time have been pronounced and there is little new in this process either in the shifts of emphasis which are recorded or the speed with which they might take place. The changing characteristics of urban neighbourhoods present a fascinating story for the urban historian. For example Peter Hall in his analysis of London has commented on the internal decay of North Kensington which traditionally 'was a working class area, which attracted new immigrants: labourers in the Acton brickfields, long since built over, whose wives took in laundry for the big houses to the south. But unlike the East End, as a community it failed to settle down; those who waxed prosperous moved out westwards, to new working class suburbs in Feltham or Southall or Hayes; their places were taken by new unskilled immigrants from Dublin or Cork, Trinidad and the Barbadoes.'[19]

Detailed studies reveal many complexities. Reeder, for example, has compared the development of Paddington in West London with that of Hammersmith.[20] Whereas Paddington became an early- and mid-Victorian residential suburb and a part of upper-middle class London, although subsequently developing symptoms of social and physical deterioration, Hammersmith failed to maintain a reputation as a fashionable Georgian suburb and was turning into a lower-middle class place of residence from the 1850s. What the urban historian has done for the understanding of past periods, is now necessary for contemporary studies.

Currently available data suggest that twilight areas present greater internal diversities than any other residential part of cities. Some areas are stable in residential occupation, perhaps with an elderly age structure; others are highly transient, with high mobility rates, and large proportions of young, one-person households. Some areas have substantial residential properties of large size, convenient for flatting and multi-occupation; others have dwellings of much smaller size, a factor which has encouraged their retention for single household occupation. Some areas have still relatively favoured environments from the point of view of space around dwellings, access to local public open space and distance from main traffic routes; others have dwellings in cramped surroundings, perhaps interspaced with workshops or factories. Some districts are essentially artisan and perhaps little changed; others, although perhaps with vestiges of middle class occupation still much in evidence, are patently in transition, and an accumulation of social difficulties together with accelerated decay of property makes for obvious problem areas. It is apparent also that certain parts of twilight areas frequently show undue concentrations of various aspects of social problems compared not only with other sectors of the urban area but also with other twilight zones.

In spite of this internal diversity, twilight zones may be thought to have a number of features which form basic characteristics. Firstly, ageing housing: here the problem is not so much unfitness (and therefore representation by the local authority as slums), but obsolescence, inadequacy of amenities, over-use and poor management. In addition to this there is a relative poverty of total environment; for example cramped housing conditions usually with limited space around dwellings, a rigid street system, poor school buildings and community facilities, lack of public open space, and an intermixture of alien land uses giving rise to problems of noise, dirt and unwanted traffic circulation.

From the social point of view these appear to be areas by and large of relative deprivation, peopled by the less well-to-do. There may be distinct socio-economic characteristics, with a relative absence of the higher social classes. With regard to housing tenure, these areas are the major concentrations of private renting (though, it may be suspected, subject to an increasing transfer to owner-occupiers).

Another common feature is that they may be considered essentially 'transitional' areas. From the physical point of view they comprise districts between clearance areas and outer rings of newer property, but they are transitional also in a social sense. Evidence suggests that particular districts are assuming new social characteristics; some are changing rapidly, some more slowly. Most obviously, districts formerly the home of the relatively affluent have been vacated by the middle class professional and business elements; some districts have become immigrant concentrations. The age structure of certain districts may have changed rapidly throwing new pressures on school provision or services for the elderly; everywhere the motor-car has invaded residential streets not suited to them.

This sort of evidence of social change, perhaps against a background of physical decay and obviously worsening environmental conditions, gives rise to social tensions in the community, between the newcomer and the residual elements in the population. The newcomer, perhaps a coloured immigrant, may have very different rules of social behaviour from the traditional resident; his expectancies of the neighbourhood and his attitudes towards it are different from his predecessor. The older resident sees his neighbourhood differently and is alarmed at the elements of change over which he has little control; his immediate world is changing too fast for him to comprehend, and there is distrust and fear of a new situation.

A final characteristic may be supposed that twilight areas perform important social functions, for example in their supply of cheap housing for a substantial number of people, particularly those with below-average incomes or above-average needs. Another residential attraction presumably is that they also allow for short journeys to work. They also might be thought to provide environments which facilitate social intercourse, but at the same time can be anonymous and provide ready accommodation for young single-person households not requiring the traditional support from local contacts. They provide accommodation areas for immigrants and those with transient housing requirements.

The complexities of twilight areas demand planning intervention of a very sophisticated kind, and here the difference between a static and an adaptive approach becomes most marked. Traditionally, local authority action in older housing areas has been through the medium of clearance and redevelopment, and in practice this has been almost a classic example of the concept and process of static planning, where a finite physical goal (with sociological assumptions) has been attained. Evidence would seem to suggest that basically the same approach is to be directed to a rehabilitation programme for houses to be improved. A programme of action is being laid down in respect of the housing stock, determined on grounds of relative fitness or unfitness, and a finite physical objective is the overriding aim.

But it is doubtful if urban renewal programmes can be entirely effective by reliance on categories of fitness. There are other relevant criteria such as function of residential area or neighbourhood, social composition and tenure system, any one or the whole of which might determine the practicability or timing of certain courses of action. These other criteria are insufficiently considered in formulating twilight area housing policies; by focussing attention on standards of fitness other very important issues are neglected. The object of renewal, as indeed is the object of planning, is not simply to obtain an improvement in physical fabric, but to achieve an improvement in total welfare.

The adaptive approach inherent in social planning at least opens a new door in this direction. In grappling with the complex problems of twilight areas, a first task is to recognize heterogeneity and, by means of social area analysis techniques, to be familiar with the socio-economic characteristics of different areas; this is quite as important as an appraisal of housing fitness and environmental quality.

These areas of creeping decay and social change require the deepest understanding to allow for the formulation of a variety of appropriate policies. A predisposition to rely upon a static planning approach will be quite inadequate for these areas, which only by a superficial analysis appear uniform and which in any case have been given a spurious standardization by concentrating on just two criteria, housing and environment. What is required is in fact an adaptive approach: one which recognizes areas where, in spite of a similarity of housing quality, there are very different social characteristics and aspirations, and where therefore no one physically oriented solution will be adequate.

Instinctive in the static approach to planning is the desire to secure uniformity by virtue of adherence to standards. In housing this is particularly apparent, and it is likely to have disastrous results as far as twilight areas are concerned because this method of renewal merely sweeps a wide variety of social problems under the carpet. The uniformity of approach to housing and environmental standardization completely fails to deal with a whole series of personal and community problems. Frequently the immediate requirements are simply to make twilight areas better places to live in, not necessarily to ensure that they are the best that technological innovation and environmental management can devise. A policy of reliance on optimum physical provision of resources, unmatched by a prior analysis of social or housing need is unlikely to make much impact on the total problem.

An adaptive planning approach would therefore differ from a static approach to the problem of twilight areas in two ways: in analysis and in implementation. A reliance on housing and environmental standards as the criteria on which to base future policies would be superseded by social area analysis, the value of which would indicate component physical and social characteristics. Secondly, the objective of attaining particular standards as requirements in improvement would be replaced by the desire to meet adequately the needs of particular communities, goals changing over time as the characteristics of particular districts change. The dynamics of the changing characteristics of twilight areas in the total urban context are much too complex for renewal to be achieved by the blunt instrument of static physical policies.

As an issue for the social planner this field is of immediate and practical importance.

Residential Migration

From the complexities surrounding the process of urban decay we may turn to urban growth. Here the key is residential mobility, both forced and unenforced; this is the medium whereby urban peripheries are extended and new communities formed.

Much too little is known of the social forces which operate in the causes of both short- and long-distance movement. Similarly, the consequences of migration are imperfectly monitored, and this lack of knowledge is apparent at both national and local level. With the redistribution of population nationally, some regions for many decades have suffered substantial out-migration and others just the reverse, but surprisingly little is known about this process beyond a broad statistical evaluation. Locally, the distribution of population at a regional or sub-regional scale has significant effects on the form and structure of urban areas, with important labour market implications, but again this does not seem to have attracted the research attention that it deserves. To cater for local movement development plans allow for a future pattern of housing supply, but rarely is the basis of that supply the subject of full analysis, taking into account for example the demographic determinants of demand, changes in housing preference and a range of locational preferences including changing attitudes to commuting.

The population profiles of people who move have been well documented in a number of studies. Migration affects certain kinds of people more readily than others, and there appear to be marked migration differentials by age, sex, status, education and many other social and demographic characteristics. For example, young adults tend to be much more migratory than older people, and there is occupational or socio-economic selectivity in favour of administrators, managers and professional workers. Migration selectivity also exists in terms of family size.

These factors underlie the causes of migration, and while local surveys will reveal particular local issues, basic theoretical frameworks should be recognized. Sjaastad[21] for example has suggested that migration takes place when the costs of migration (both money and non-money costs) are equal to or less than the difference in the present value of the benefits at the points of origin and destination.

Alternately, Rossi[22] has seen mobility as a process whereby families adjust their housing to the housing needs generated by the shifts in family composition that accompany life cycle changes.

There are important underlying issues in the reasons for migration. Relevant supporting data has recently been given by a survey of migration in the Northern Region, where it was claimed that reasons for movement could be broadly grouped into motivations which were 'home-centred' and those which were 'area-centred'.[23] For people moving very short distances (less than fifty minutes' walk) 'home-centred' motivations were the most important. For example, there were reasons concerned with domestic amenities: the desire for a home with additional or improved indoor facilities and the desire for a larger home, either in the form of larger rooms or more rooms (or both), were the most significant. Another important factor concerned tenure: many respondents in the survey gave as their reason for movement the wish to be an owner-occupier. Changes in household composition were another reason.

On the other hand for people moving longer distances, especially either out of or into the region, 'area-centred' motivations were dominant. For in-migrants previous ties with the North were important, but employment factors formed major influences. The lack of suitable employment was an even more important reason for out-migrants, but the strength of previous ties with the newly selected region was understandably of less significance.

Migration is a very normal activity to most households, occurring on average perhaps every two or three years during the peak years of twenty to forty, and it is precisely at this time of household formation and rapid change in occupational rewards that critical decisions are made regarding choices in housing and its location. Studies of population migration identifying the 'pushes' and the 'pulls' which determine movement, together with studies of housing demand, are therefore as significant as any for the planner concerned with identifying pressures in urban expansion. The demand for owner-occupation and the question of housing preferences by type of dwelling and location would seem to be critical issues for investigation; certainly, constraints in these fields are likely to be very damaging from the point of view of attainment of residential satisfaction.

An interesting facet of migration is the recognition of a 'migratory elite'. Musgrove for example has argued that internal movement in Britain is a process whereby the population is resorted into socially homogeneous groups, with socially divisive rather than cohesive results.[24] He argued that significant changes making for elite migration date from the 1860s; at that time a variety of converging economic and social developments began to detach the professional, managerial and white-collar worker from local ties. With the growing availability of educational facilities, a man's personal and perhaps local background has been replaced by his technical competence as the major factor for his success in business and professional life. Musgrove's survey of a Midland city in 1960 illustrated the point: in professional occupations in particular (senior local government officers and grammar school heads) immigrants were markedly over-represented to locally born people. The proportion of those in the professional occupations who came from cities of 100,000 inhabitants or more was much higher than could be expected from the proportion of big city people to total population. This is added evidence of the great forces which lead to concentrations of economic, social and political power in large urban areas.

In spite of the dislocations consequent upon migration there may well be favourable attitudes towards movement, especially with professional persons where migration is necessary for advancement. It all depends whether positive attitudinal and emotional adaptations to movement can be forged. It is in the public sector where the adverse aspects of migration have been commented upon, especially where enforced movement with redevelopment has been involved. Forced dislocation can be a highly disruptive and disturbing experience; Fried has spoken of it as 'grieving for a lost home', commenting that losses generally bring about fragmentation of routines, of relationships, of expectations and imply an alteration in the world of physically available objects and spatially overted action.[25]

These psychological aspects of relocation have their very practical significance. From the heart of a redevelopment area in Birmingham, Ladywood, Canon Norman Power pleads for his 'forgotten people': 'Is it possible,' he asks, 'for our planners moving the models on their boards to consider the feelings of a child from an insecure home whose only chance of affection is a stable relationship with an understanding teacher.'[26] This raises altogether different considerations from the question of migration and its underlying causes and consequences, but the fact is that for the planner a related practical problem is to be found in redevelopment areas and the disruption of existing communities.

Environment and Communities

The relationship between environment and behaviour has long been a matter of considerable relevance for planning. It is an issue which extends deep into the philosophical origins of planning and because of the impact of the practical experiments conducted during the nineteenth century under the influence of this philosophy it is still a factor in planning questions today. The traditional theme has been that unsatisfactory residential environments promote community disharmony and are the starting point for crime and anti-social behaviour. The antidote has been to remedy the physical environment for community happiness to be fostered and for old social problems to disappear.

The crudity of this approach is of course not now followed, but the issue is still a live one. Part of the planner's task is to create new environments and control adverse change in existing ones, constantly exploring possibilities for improvement; where residential areas are concerned the nature or quality of the physical environment is claimed to be critical in determining community satisfaction. Improvement in environment is constantly sought, but what criteria constitute improvement? What features of the physical environment are most significant from the social point of view? When is the social environment more pertinent than the physical environment as the basis for promoting satisfactory living conditions? What social results stem from housing at different densities? What are the social consequences of different types of residential layout? When and how is social intercourse hindered or fostered? Under what conditions is multi-occupation an unsatisfactory form of living? How much overcrowding can be reasonably withstood?

There are many such social questions which are very relevant for the planner. Space does not permit an adequate examination of all the issues, but to illustrate the complexities which are involved we might select one topic as an example. This is overcrowding, and it serves to indicate the sort of new fields in which the specialist social planner might become concerned.[27]

Overcrowding and Behaviour

Overcrowding has long been considered together with bad housing as a root cause of social problems, especially in big cities, and in spite of long-standing improvements it is by no means an issue which planners may conveniently ignore. The worst examples of overcrowding occur in central London, but in addition Mersey-side, the West Midlands and Tyneside have overcrowding comparable to Scotland and Northern Ireland, areas where the highest proportions of overcrowded households are to be found.

During the nineteenth century, overcrowding was tackled by the definition of space standards. These were applied to hospital wards, army barracks, prisons, workhouses and common lodging houses, and calculated from the amount of oxygen consumed by an individual and the expected rate of air change in the room. On the other hand, standards for family houses were not embodied in statutes, but housing reformers erected 'model dwellings', with the hope that private builders would copy them.

While the underlying principle may have been the maintenance of public health, the social reformers of the day also recognized a moral danger in overcrowding. For example, the regulations governing the occupancy of common lodging houses required that persons of opposite sex above the age of ten, other than married couples, should sleep in separate rooms. Observers had been struck by the apparent relationship between overcrowding and the growth and concentration of immorality, crime and ill-health, a point constantly seized on by the moralists of the day.

The general situation regarding densities and overcrowding in this country is now much improved. Between 1845 and 1965 the overall floor space in London increased at the rate of about one square foot every two years, with innovations such as a separate bathroom, more space for storage and circulation and the development of the kitchen. Nevertheless, overcrowding of dwellings, exacerbated by multi-occupation, still remains obstinately characteristic of many parts of our towns and cities, and it is right to recognize that in spite of the very encouraging improvements which have taken place, particular localized concentrations do still exist.

On the face of it there are some extremely disturbing indications as to the effect of overcrowding. There is the work, for example, of scientists investigating population density and social pathology through experience concerning the toleration of density in rats and mice. Where genetically similar mice are put into groups of the same size into boxes of similar size and are left alone to struggle for food supply, then their response to crowding is destructive—murder, killing of the young and perversions of behaviour. The controlled experiments of John Calhoun and John Christian are notable in this respect.

Calhoun's experiments were on a domestic albino strain of the Norway rat.[28] Groups were permitted to increase to approximately twice the number that experience indicated could occupy the available space with only moderate stress from social interaction.

> The consequences of the behavioural pathology we observed were most apparent among the females. Many were unable to carry pregnancy to full term or to survive delivery of their litters if they did. An even greater number after successfully giving birth, fell short in their maternal functions. Among the males, the behaviour disturbances ranged from sexual deviation to cannibalism and from frenetic overactivity to a pathological withdrawal from which individuals would emerge to eat, drink and move about only when other members of the community were asleep. The social organization of the animals showed equal disruption. Each of the experimental populations divided itself into several groups, in each of which the sex ratios were drastically modified.

Has this relevance for the planner, concerned as he is with crowded cities, where there are also perversions of human behaviour?

There is of course a relationship of a kind between the physical environment and behaviour. Where there is lack of space in the home for example, families must inevitably feel cramped. If kitchens are to be used for meals then a standard of ninety square feet may be inadequate; seventy square feet for a bedroom is also inadequate if it is to accommodate reasonably sized furniture. Storage is a big problem. Space-consuming hobbies are particularly prejudiced, and there may be inadequate space for drying clothes. Noise disturbance is a serious problem, and externally there is lack of space for children's play.

There are particular effects of crowding on the individual. For example there may be positive health correlations. Infectious diseases may ensue from the multiple use of toilet and water facilities; digestive diseases may be related to the inadequate storage of food. There may be injuries stemming from home accidents because of crowded kitchens. There may be inadequate heating and ventilation and poor sleeping arrangements leading to fatigue, irritation and unproductive expenditure of energy. In this way overcrowding contributes to general strain and stress on people, and in the words of James Plant:

Plate I   Proposed Model Town of Victoria from 'National Evils and Practical
Remedies' (J. S. Buckingham) (*By courtesy of the City Librarian, Sheffield*)

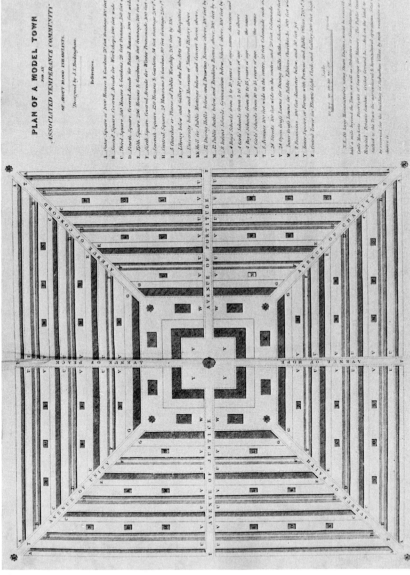

Plate II   Plan of a Model Town for an Associated Temperance Community of
about 10,000 inhabitants from 'National Evils and Practical Remedies'
(J. S. Buckingham) (*By courtesy of the City Librarian, Sheffield*)

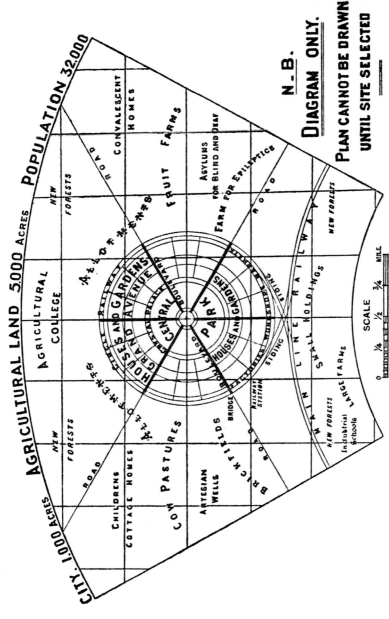

GARDEN - CITY

CITY. 1,000 ACRES

AGRICULTURAL LAND 5,000 ACRES   POPULATION 32,000

N_B.
DIAGRAM ONLY.
PLAN CANNOT BE DRAWN
UNTIL SITE SELECTED

CONVALESCENT HOMES

FRUIT FARMS

ASYLUMS FOR BLIND AND DEAF
FARM FOR EPILEPTICS

NEW FORESTS

AGRICULTURAL COLLEGE

WARD & CENTRE

GRAND AVENUE

HOUSES AND GARDENS

CENTRAL PARK

HOUSES AND GARDENS

WARD & CENTRE

BOULEVARD

NEW FORESTS

NEW FORESTS

ROAD

ROAD

ROAD

SIDING

RAILWAY

MAIN LINE RAILWAY

SMALL HOLDINGS

LARGE FARMS

Industrial
Schools

NEW FORESTS

RAILWAY STATION

BRIDGE

BRICKFIELDS

ARTESIAN WELLS

COW PASTURES

CHILDRENS COTTAGE HOMES

NEW FORESTS

ROAD

SCALE
0   ¼   ½   ¾   MILE

Plate III   Garden City and Rural Belt from 'Garden Cities of Tomorrow'
(E. Howard) (By courtesy of Faber and Faber)

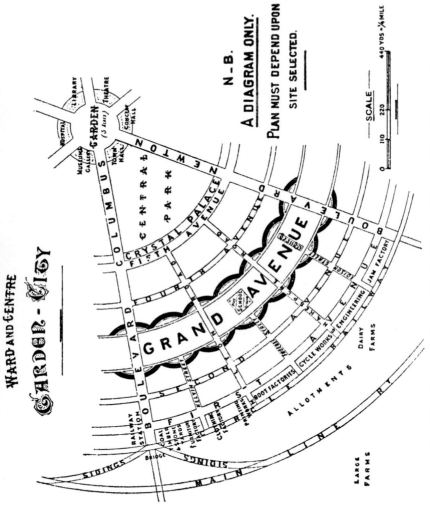

Plate IV   Ward and Centre of Garden City from 'Garden Cities of Tomorrow' (E. Howard) (By courtesy of Faber and Faber)

Plate V   Sparkbrook, Birmingham: The Newcomers
(*By courtesy of the Birmingham Post*)

Plate VI   Killingworth New Township: pedestrian way and children's play space
(*By courtesy of the Director of Development, Killingworth*)

Plate VII   Park Hill, Sheffield (*By courtesy of the City Architect, Sheffield*)

Plate VIII   Rye Hill, Newcastle upon Tyne: artist's impression, 'before'
(*By courtesy of the City Planning Officer, Newcastle upon Tyne*)

Plate IX   Rye Hill, Newcastle upon Tyne: artist's impression, 'after'
(*By courtesy of the City Planning Officer, Newcastle upon Tyne*)

Plate X   Sparkbrook, Birmingham: Claremont Road
(By courtesy of the Birmingham Post)

When we realize that for many of these individuals from one year's end to the other, there is never a time that they are alone, we begin to get some picture of what this tension must be. Even the nights conspire to the same end; three to five children sleeping in the same bed means that even during the periods of relaxation and for the deeper levels of the unconscious there must always be this awareness of the imminence of others and the compromises and surrenders which this entails [29]

There are also psychological effects. Periods of being alone, and of having the privacy of one's own room are all-important in fostering a feeling of individuality and self-sufficiency. This is particularly important in respect of children, because persistent crowding from early life may destroy the sense of individuality and their very ability to be alone. Moreover, among constantly crowded families there may be the phenomenon of being so much in the world that there is no chance to look at it from the outside; one's capacity for objectivity is prejudiced in these circumstances and an important factor in life is lost.

There is now a wealth of statistical evidence on the relation of environment, including the particular question of overcrowding, on health. Certain infectious diseases tend to occur at earlier ages in overcrowded surroundings, and it has long been demonstrated that overcrowding per room, and to a lesser extent density of housing per acre, shows an independent positive association with mortality. However, in spite of the long tradition of statistical investigations it is wise not to attach too much importance to studies carried out in the past, for there has been such a continued improvement in the health and social conditions of the population over the last decades, that the relative importance of the various factors influencing the health of the community has changed. For example, previously a family close to starvation might be particularly prone to the effects of overcrowding and poor environment. Now however the same overcrowding might have little effect because of the considerably reduced level of malnutrition and the wider social and medical services available.

One can suggest therefore that crowding and very high densities may have physical and psychological consequences for households and the individual. The difficulty about all this is the problem of measuring the relationship of this particular aspect of the environment on behaviour generally, and the isolation of crowding from all the other criteria with which it is commonly associated. In fact

D

it is the effect of the *total* physical and social environment in which the planner may be more interested.

This is so because of the interrelationship of all the factors concerned: social class, occupational status, unemployment, poverty, mental capacity, general ability, social and health education of parents, all of which might interact for a particular family within the setting of a physical environment.

Surveys in many large cities have shown that social defects are localized, with frequent concentrations in inner residential areas noted for a number of characteristics, including overcrowding. But it is difficult to isolate overcrowding itself as a factor in promoting social problems. In Sainsbury's study of suicide in London for example, suicide rates increased in areas of overcrowding but only when they were areas of social disorganization.[30] Similarly, in Philp's survey of problem families, nearly one third of his sample were overcrowded, but then there are many other factors which make for problem families.[31] In planning research work in Newcastle, overcrowding was certainly shown to have dramatic correlations with the incidence of 'social malaise', but there were other positive correlations too.[32]

Behaviour is in fact the product of a vast complex of factors. Titmuss has commented on these lines regarding the delinquent area of central Liverpool.

> Out of a long history of poverty, neglect and exploitation, culturally transmitted from generation to generation, there has accumulated a tradition of delinquent behaviour. Such behaviour is for the majority of these boys not so much a manifestation of individual maladjustment but is part of the total process of adjustment to a sub-culture in conflict with the culture of society as a whole.[33]

The point emerges that overcrowding is just *one* element in a whole range of poor housing conditions including unfitness, noise, vermin and environmental deprivation, and it is very difficult to isolate that or indeed any particular factor in its effect on behaviour.

So in short the question of overcrowding and human behaviour might be considered at two levels. First are the more obvious effects on he behaviour of an individual or group; these may be direct, as on health, or indirect, having longer-term psychological consequences. Second are the impersonal, indirect influences in association with a host of interrelated social and environmental factors and a particular cultural background which can promote individual behaviour at variance with traditionally accepted values of society at large.

The first of these influences can as a rule be measured, providing evidence to show the ill-effect of overcrowding. In this way, more acceptable densities in problem areas of our cities will be achieved. This will point the way to what practical limits might be put to density levels. On the other hand of course the trend towards declining densities is likely in any case to continue; enhanced material prosperity is accompanied by the demand for greater space standards throughout society.

The wider, indirect effects of overcrowding pose more difficulties for the planner and open up further questions. The concentration of social problems in particular sectors of our urban areas can readily be demonstrated, but the more important effects of high residential densities and overcrowding are so interconnected with other aspects of poor housing conditions or characteristics of the social environment that the search to identify casual relationships will not be particularly profitable. But a continual concern for the effects of overcrowding is necessary: the problem will never be eradicated and its effects will always bear on those least able to withstand it. As a feature of city life it is here to stay in one form or other and will remain an issue in the wide field of social planning.

Urban Decay and Social Organization

The two Censuses of 1961 and 1966, through their provision of data for small areas (Enumeration Districts), have afforded new possibilities for planners to evaluate certain aspects of the socio-economic and physical structure of urban areas. In this way a meaningful and fairly accurate picture of the component structure of towns and cities can be prepared at remarkably little cost and involving no additional survey work by the local authority.

Distinctive spatial patterns with extremes of advantaged and disadvantaged neighbourhoods characterize most urban areas. On the one hand the Census data will reveal districts featured for example by owner-occupation, low occupancy rates, high car ownership, large proportions of persons in managerial, professional or administrative occupations and where there is a marked tendency for children to stay on at school after fifteen. On the other hand there are districts characterized by private renting, high occupancy rates, shared accommodation, shared or absent facilities such as toilets or cooking stove, a high frequency of residential turnover, a substantial proportion of the total population foreign born, above-average unemployment, an unskilled population and a high proportion of early school leavers. For an understanding of the internal social structure of urban areas the planner should make exhaustive use of Census material, as the basis for more detailed neighbourhood studies.

The spatial pattern of environmental criteria from the Census can be augmented by that of social defects with data collected from other sources. Just as we have advantaged and disadvantaged neighbourhoods from the socio-economic and physical points of view, so we have privileged and deprived neighbourhoods in terms of social organization. Concentrations of particular defects have long been recognized, but, symptomatic of the planner's traditional lack of interest in social characteristics in favour of physical criteria, this aspect of total environment has been neglected in the formulation of social planning policies.

As early as 1925 Burt showed with regard to juvenile delinquency in London for example that the highest rates were located in areas which were adjacent to the central districts of the city, with the lowest rates occurring near the periphery. In 1934 the Social Survey of Merseyside revealed an accumulation of such social defects as mental deficiency, deafness, blindness, tuberculosis, immorality, crime, alcoholism and chronic destitution in the inner areas of Liverpool. In 1942 the Chicago studies of juvenile delinquency in urban areas were recorded, again confirming concentrations in the central zone with progressive declines to the outer zones.[34]

These are only a number of early studies indicating that accumulations of social defects existed within specific areas of large cities, and suggesting the profitability of this form of ecological research. The general findings from these and subsequent studies show that the incidence of delinquency, crime, mental illness and suicide has been found to be highest in the central districts and the immediate surroundings. Beyond this the incidence of deviant behaviour declines, but the pattern in any particular city is markedly complicated by variations in the composition of the population by such as age, sex, marital status, social class, ethnic origins and religious affiliation.

Therefore the planning of all major urban areas would clearly benefit from individual studies because of the importance of the detail revealed at the local level. Some such studies have already paved the way in clarifying research methods. In Hobart, Tasmania, there has been a study of the distribution of delinquency, where in post-war years there has been a strong tendency for the concentration to shift from the inner areas to fringe government-housing areas.[35] In Exeter, it has been found that two-fifths of the juvenile delinquents reside in a single ward, an out-of-town council estate erected in the 1930s.[36] In Liverpool an investigation of social defects has concerned mental defectiveness, mental illness, children in care and children on probation, with a view to studying the distribution in terms of family breakdown and its treatment through administrative processes; the relationship between the incidence of social defects and various stages of city growth was confirmed.[37]

These studies are important issues for the planner in that they illustrate the sociological aspects of urban decay. Because he is not solely concerned with the physical aspects of decay and renewal, but in planning for the total welfare of the community, this represents a vital, relevant field of interest. These investigations have focussed attention on a wide range of social problems which exist primarily in the inner areas of cities, not only the redevelopment districts but also those twilight areas reserved for housing improvement. Hints have been made of a slum sub-culture or of a state of social disorganization. The importance of this is simply that physical planning policies in the field of housing, whether clearance or rehabilitation, are constrained by, and should be formulated in the light of, serious social questions. The community concerned has problems which cannot remotely be solved through the medium of housing improvement alone; neither is their solution made any easier by the divorce of housing and planning policies from other aspects of social welfare—this is the new co-ordination which is demanded.

There are of course different types of residential decay and the problems they pose are far from similar. One area of decay is characterized by a large spread of small, artisan houses; in some cities, notably in Scotland, the Victorian tenement is the main feature; elsewhere decay has set in in areas of formerly middle class occupation where large houses may now be sub-divided. Very often it is the latter type of area which has emerged as the main social problem area of cities.

These problem areas are notorious for high concentrations of social blight or 'malaise', although even in the worst, social disorganization extends to only a small minority of the total population. It is necessary for the planner to isolate and identify these critical areas so that social planning objectives may be keyed in with the aims of physical planning schemes.

The process of decay and the part played by social, economic and physical factors, is imperfectly understood. The critical factors which promote decay and the emergence of social problem areas will certainly differ in detail from city to city, but as far as the concentration of social blight is concerned, the notion of 'drift' of a certain type of person, including those with psychological abnormalities, to these areas is one which might be investigated. Meanwhile the practical issue at stake is that social problem areas provide a refuge for those who find it difficult if not impossible to secure or qualify for better accommodation elsewhere.

Whatever the factors in their emergence these residual areas frequently come into prominence over a fairly short span of years; as a new element in the urban social structure they can build up relatively quickly by processes of filtering and invasion and succession, whereby housing is passed down the social scale. This is characteristically so where formerly well-to-do areas in the inner suburbs are rapidly deserted by traditional middle-class occupances in favour of newcomers of quite different status. Because of their geographical location where physical renewal objectives are to be concentrated in the next decades, the areas will constantly be to the forefront in overall planning problems. This demands constant vigilance by the planner in the monitoring of change in the inner areas of cities and a much deeper understanding of the factors involved; only in this way is he going to make a contribution to the total planning process.

Many of the inner transitional areas manage to contain their problems and to withstand the effects of disadvantaged environments; here social disorganization is held at bay. But a very small number become true residual areas ('sumps') and increasingly are excluded from the normal community beyond. The process seems to act like a downward spiral of confidence; barriers of stratification are extended and it becomes harder rather than easier to escape. Frequently poverty becomes the key, itself a syndrome of mutually reinforcing handicaps. Ultimately, a problem sub-culture might be identified where the whole area subscribes to a set of values different from those held in the wider society, although this must be thought to be very rare in view of the short time span which is usually involved.

Throughout the process of social selection or rejection in which certain households move out and others move in, an area of minimum choice with low standards becomes peopled by the gravitation of a critical number (although very much in a minority) of families characterized by stress and strain of one form or another. In this process the importance of individual family functioning has been noted. It has been argued that some families, 'integrative' by nature, seem to provide a secure framework and can contain stress within the boundary of the family and deal with it from their own resources. On the other hand there are 'disintegrative' families where there is a wide discrepancy between the internal values of the family and the values of the outside world, and where there is reliance on outside help and a wider kinship group. In these differences, the distinctive feature is the nature of the fit between the roles of spouses: this is the 'marital fit' which seems to constitute the decisive influence on whether the symptoms of stress within can or cannot be contained.[38]

Into such issues the planner is led in his concern to understand the functioning of communities in respect of which he is preparing policies. Needless to say, much more research work is needed concerning residual areas: the issues in physical urban decay, the gravitation of social problems to particular districts, and the relationship between the physical and social environments. As an example of the sort of work which can make an important contribution for the planning team, we might refer to a recent study conducted in Newcastle upon Tyne.[39]

This concerned the collection of a wide range of data, in the form of home addresses, in respect of physical, social and mental ill-health for the City, largely for 1963–4, as follows: deaths from bronchitis, pneumonia and lung cancer, notifications of respiratory tuberculosis, still births and perinatal deaths, suicide, illegitimate births, venereal infection, persons found guilty of 'offences against the person' (sexual, wounding and assaults), larceny and 'offences against property' (burglary, housebreaking, breaking and entering), persons on probation, juvenile delinquents, persons receiving National Assistance, cases dealt with by social workers, psychiatric cases, mentally sub-normal persons, and child neglect.

This data was analysed to show the relationship with certain selected aspects of the physical and social environment as given in the 1961 Census. To illustrate this in the context of the previous section, one of these was overcrowding, represented by occupancy rates.

The statistical method of analysis was to record the incidence of each aspect of social malaise, listed above, in each Enumeration District of the Census; the 371 E.Ds. in the City which contain private households were divided into three groups of more or less equal number. This gives, again for example with over-crowding, a group of 120 E.Ds. with the most overcrowding, the next 120 E.Ds., and finally the remaining 131 E.Ds. with least overcrowding. In this way one can calculate the differential incidence of, say, bronchitis deaths or suicide or juvenile delin-quents between the worst or the least overcrowded third of the City.

A refinement in the analysis took into account the varying age structures in particular districts. This is necessary because for example a high juvenile delinquency rate might be unduly influenced by a high proportion of juveniles, or a high bronchitis death rate by a high proportion of old persons in the district concerned. The resulting 'refined' ratio suggested the degree of correlation with those aspects of the social and physical environ-ment selected.

The interim conclusions from this work were positive and striking. It was readily demonstrated that there are strong correla-tions between the distribution of indices of physical, social and mental ill-health and indices of the social and physical environ-ment. Occasionally the relationships are marginal but with every index of ill-health there is at least one relationship which is marked. The force of the relationships is given greater significance because the pattern of distribution of total environmental prob-lems throughout Newcastle fits almost exactly the pattern of dis-tribution of ill-health problems. As environmental problems increase so generally does the level of social malaise, but a parti-cular residual area of blight was identified immediately west of the central area, known locally under the generic name of Rye Hill.

Of the five physical and social environment variables, over-crowding showed the most dramatic correlations with the aspects of social malaise. With regard to physical ill-health, notifications of respiratory tuberculosis in the most overcrowded third of the City were twice those in the least overcrowded third; perinatal deaths were forty-three per cent higher in the most overcrowded third. Venereal disease was five times more prevalent in the most overcrowded third of the City; offences against the person also showed the same proportion, while that for larceny was only a little less. Persons on probation were seven times more numerous and juvenile delinquents three times more numerous in the most overcrowded third of the City than the least overcrowded. Cases of child neglect were five to six times greater in this sector of the City, and mentally sub-normal persons were three times more numerous.

These findings however do not provide an answer to the origin of the problem, namely the nature of the relationship between environment and behaviour. An accumulation of problems in one particular area cannot be held to prove that they have arisen as a connected process of cause and effect. The belief that social blight is no more than the inevitable consequences of slum conditions or a particular aspect of urban decay is far too simple. The need for further ecological studies is clear and for planning both to draw on and contribute to further interdisciplinary research in this field.

Mental Health

This section on environment and the community concludes with another issue for the planner, namely mental health. This is an important field of concern especially in the planning of new communities where there is the question of 'suburban neurosis' or more recently 'new town blues'. The planner is helped by a number of recent studies and he should be familiar with their findings, contradictory though some of them may appear.

A survey of mental illness by Martin, Brotherston and Chave (1957) was carried out in a new housing estate about twelve miles from London.[40] The estate, called Outlands by the authors, had been built by the London County Council betwen 1948 and 1952 and planned as a dormitory suburb. There was limited accommodation for social organizations. The 16,500 population had moved there from all parts of Greater London and the majority had lived formerly in very inadequate accommodation. The mental health survey found that the mental hospital admission rate was about fifty per cent above the national level, anxiety neurosis was twice as high and self-reported nervous symptoms eighty per cent above the national figures. From this evidence it was concluded that mental illness, particularly in its neurotic manifestations, was more prevalent on the estate than in the country as a whole. Possible precipitating factors such as he attenuation of kinship ties, social isolation and the economic stresses resulting from removal to a new area were suspected contributory causes, but this was speculation only.

This evidence was tested in a later survey, also in the London area. A New Town, given the fictitious name of Newton, was selected. With a population of 40,000 by 1959, more than half the families had come from the Greater London area; these represented a relatively wide cross-section of the social classes with a much smaller working class element than Outlands. A small control study area in that area of London from where most of the residents had originated was given the name of Oldfield.

The mental health surveys had interesting results. First of all sub-clinical neurosis: its incidence was found to be virtually the same in an old London borough, in an out-country estate without local work or social life, and in a planned new town. Here then was a disease entity with its roots deep in the physical or emotional background of the individual: a product not of the immediate environment, but 'constitutional' in that it represents a deeply embedded pattern within the nervous system. On the other hand, with regard to psychoses, the New Town rates for both psychiatric out-patients and in-patients were below the national figures, whereas the out-country estate rates in both cases were above the national figures. This suggested to the authors that good social planning can reduce the incidence of psychosis, whereas bad social planning or lack of it can do the reverse.

Another survey of comparisons has been carried out in Croydon, in respect of the mental health of persons on a new estate with that of persons living in an older area.[41] The survey method included a household interview survey, a study of general practitioners' records, and a study of hospital cases. In this case a principal result was that for the great majority of indices of mental health, no difference was found in the prevalence of mental health between the two sample populations. Where there were differences, these seemed most readily explicable in terms of demographic or geographic factors. The authors concluded that 'as no important difference was found between the mental health of the two populations, then either the lack of social amenities on the new estate had no measurable effect on mental health, or, in so far as it had an adverse effect, this was balanced by a beneficial effect of other factors'.

In these studies, the social issues of town planning take us into the field of socio-medical investigations. The relevance of these do not stop with mental health. Loneliness is another important issue, not only for young housebound wives on new estates but for the elderly in old neighbourhoods. Loneliness as a problem is found not only in new areas, where it has been particularly investigated, but also in older urban areas. It may increase as families are split into small groups and as physical mobility increases; it may also increase with the age of people, old age being a time of diminishing social contacts and domestic support. Some loneliness may be an inherent defect requiring medical treatment: a Newcastle study found that 'bereavement, reduction in contacts and physical disability are not in themselves sufficient causes of psychiatric illness; their traumatic effects depend on a pre-existing vulnerability'.[42] Once again it can readily be demonstrated therefore that physical planning policies (in this case, for example, concerning the nature of a residential layout designed to promote social intercourse) cannot be divorced from an awareness of personal and community factors which draw on the widest sociological knowledge.

The development of a specialist social planning approach clearly demands the closest links with interdisciplinary studies on the broadest front. Take the phenomenon of suicide for example. No one single cause or group of causes can account for the level of suicide rates. They have been found to be positively correlated with male sex, increasing age, widowhood, single and divorced state, childlessness, high density of population, residence in big towns and in particular urban sectors, a high standard of living, economic crisis, alcohol consumption, a history of a broken home in childhood, mental disorder, and physical illness. The planner, inasmuch as he contributes to the shaping of the environment, might well contribute unwittingly to the incidence of this phenomenon; if so, he has a role to play in any conceived remedies by contributing to a pool of professional skills drawn from many different sources.

Stengel, writing on suicide, has discussed the 'therapeutic community' thus:

> . . . the responsibility for those in need of psychological and social therapy would no longer be monopolized by the expert, as is the case now, but by a network of lay persons aware of their roles as helpers to those in need. . . . The invocation of moral principles propounded by religious and other philosophies will have to be supplemented by the expert knowledge which psychiatrists, social psychologists and sociologists have already to offer and which they will have to expand rapidly. . . . The planning, organization and running of an all-embracing social service in which every member of

the community plays a role which is meaningful to him, is the great challenge of modern society.[43]

Planning has a part to play in this social service; the development of social planning will facilitate this.

The Underprivileged

Almost any social study is of relevance to the planner, however oblique some of them might be without a full appreciation of what is involved. This is so with studies of particular sections of society. To select some of these such as the problem family, the very poor and the immigrant, will illustrate the point: issues surrounding these groups are relevant to the planner simply because planning policies which are concerned with the environment cannot be adequately framed without cognizance of their problems.

Problem Families

The common characteristics of problem families are first of all their inability to cope with demands made upon them, and secondly their resultant need to fall back to an excessive degree on statutory and voluntary help. Their difficulties are made manifest in a number of ways: inadequate housing, irregular and largely insufficient income, inadequate home care, neglect of children, mental ill-health and personality disorders, emotional and behaviour difficulties and unstable personal relationships. With these characteristics problem families have been objects of study and concern as sociological phenomena; rarely however have they formed the basis of an exercise in social planning.

One exception to this has been in Newcastle where a working party which investigated the situation in that city included a variety of different officers: the Legal Adviser, the Medical Officer, Director of Education, Director of Housing, Children's Officer and the Planning Officer.[44] As an interdepartmental study this was an example of the contributory role the planner can play both in an examination of a particular problem and subsequent policy formulation.

The situation in 1965 was that from the point of view of the Director of Housing there were particular concentrations of 'low-grade' families in certain areas of Newcastle, and it was being found difficult to promote housing and environmental improvement and to engage in social remedial work because of the tendency of these families to support and encourage each other against authority. The significance of the concentrations was also that the pattern of problem family distribution was strongly correlated with deficiencies or irregularities of the physical and social environment as suggested by the Census, and similarly with the incidence a social malaise (see pp. 93-4). It was found that in most cases problem families were at least several times more susceptible to aspects of social ill-health than were non-problem families, and that this was particularly so in the case of crime.

A planning research study was therefore able to show the facts of location and to point to a relationship with total environmental problems. It immediately became clear that any comprehensive attempt as a co-ordinated measure between the local authority, voluntary services, the churches and individual social workers to provide a remedial service for problem families had to be conceived in very wide terms. Support could not be seen as a special service designed to meet specific problems, for example child care, family planning or domestic help, but as help for the people who formed the families, with all their situational difficulties and personality deficiencies.

Deep social problems like these are community problems because the roots which nourish the problems lie outside the individual: they are to be found in the family, in society and in the environment in which they live. The planner is concerned with that environment and therefore should be considered as part of the community work team concerned with this and related issues. As Philp remarks: 'These [parents] are vulnerable people in an exposed situation. Measures to help them must first and foremost be general social measures which will give to everyone in the community the opportunity of employment, decent housing, freedom from poverty, care in sickness and the chance of as full a life as possible. . . .'[45]

Poverty

In just the same way the issue of poverty is not one that can be isolated for either study or remedy, because as a problem it both contributes to and is supported by a large number of other factors. Many of these are environmental in the broadest sense, and again the town planner might contribute to both an analysis of the situation and an approach towards solutions.

The despairing feature about poverty is that it is self-perpetuating.

The children of the poor and ill-educated start school at a disadvantage, and soon fall behind. Their parents can give them little help or encouragement; school becomes a humiliating experience, where they cannot meet the teacher's demands, and finally lose her interest. They take the first opportunity to drop out. Without skills or confidence in themselves, they remain marginally employable. Some work off their frustration in crime and violence, most will always be poor. Robbed of the self-respect that comes from earning a decent livelihood, the young men cannot sustain the responsibilities of marriage, and so they bequeath to their children the same burden of ignorance, broken homes and apathy by which they were themselves crippled.[46]

It is difficult to identify the extent of poverty but a recent survey has indicated that 18 per cent of the households (14 per cent of the persons) in the United Kingdom, representing nearly 7,500,000 persons, were living in 1960 below a defined 'National Assistance' level of living.[47] The authors' analysis contradicts the view that a trend towards greater equality has accompanied the trend towards greater affluence. One of their significant findings was the extent of poverty among children; for over a decade it was generally assumed that such poverty as exists was found overwhelmingly among the aged, but quantitatively the problem of poverty now among children is more than two-thirds of the size of poverty among the aged. The authors' findings were that 5–6 per cent of the population in 1960 were in low-income households because wages, even when supplemented by family allowances, were insufficient to raise them above the minimum level. A further 3–4 per cent were in households receiving social insurance benefits (chiefly pensions) but the latter were insufficient. A further 4–5 per cent of the population were in low-income households because under various regulations they were not entitled to the full scale of National Assistance grant or because the minimum the authors have taken is considerably above the basic National Assistance scale.

A recent survey of a particular locality seems to confirm these findings.[48] More than a third of the families interviewed on a Nottingham council estate of 650 houses have been reported to be living in poverty, with 37 per cent of the families having incomes of less than £14 per week and 57 per cent with less than £20. Again, a disturbing factor was the predominance of children under 15 years of age: more than two-fifths of those in poverty were children.

Surveys like these are necessary to discover who are the poor, where they are, how many of them there are and what kind of assistance they need. In this way, poverty as a fact of society and a concern for all those determined to provide equality of opportunity must lie at the heart of any social policy. Neglect of interest during the 1950s is now being remedied, and poverty is becoming, with housing, a major issue in community planning.

The difficulty of making an impact on the problem is well known. In America for example a generation separates two Democratic Presidents both of whom have declared their faith in, and intent on achieving improvement. 'The test of our progress is not whether we add more to the abundance of those who have much,' declared Franklin D. Roosevelt; 'it is whether we provide enough for those who have too little.' For Lyndon B. Johnson, 'The war on poverty is not a struggle simply to support people, to make them dependent on the generosity of others. It is a struggle to give people a chance. It is an effort to allow them to develop and use their capacities, as we have been allowed to develop and use ours, so that they can share, as others share, in the promise of this nation.'[49]

This struggle to narrow the gap between abundance and poverty is an essential social issue for the town planner. Realistic policy formulation will require detailed social studies, both urban- and rural-based, to discover the factors involved in perpetuating and indeed increasing the incidence of poverty. The planner should be able to play an important role here with his concern for environment and total community problems.

The Immigrant

As a further example of underprivilege in the community we might instance the coloured immigrant. Compared with the problem family and the question of poverty there has been a relatively large literary output in recent years about the immigrant. There have been for example the publications of the National Committee for Commonwealth Immigrants, observations from national surveys such as the PEP *Report on Racial Discrimination* and more local studies such as the Sparkbrook (Birmingham) investigation *Race, Community and Conflict*. A host of reports allows us to be better informed than ever before, but the town planner might argue that wide research fields have still only been tentatively explored.

The immigrant is a new factor in the range of contemporary

social issues which concern the planner. While the immigrant adds a new dimension to the fusion of cultures and backgrounds which compose city life (Plate V), he poses problems by virtue of residential concentrations by and large in those areas of towns disadvantaged from the point of view of housing and environment. We have argued that in the comprehensive range of policies which are adopted for these areas, the character of the community is a crucial element for consideration; in many of the larger cities the immigrant as well as the host community will be included.

Most studies of immigrant groups have been sociological in nature, and the planner has not so far played a prominent role in area or community investigations. An exception to this has been at Newcastle where an immigrant research worker (a sociologist who had had practical experience in an Indian Planning Office) was employed in the City Planning Department during 1966 and 1967 for the express purpose of making a study of the local immigrant situation.

The general brief was to investigate the immigrants' underlying community tensions and their problems with regard to housing and social conditions. To narrow the field somewhat the study was concerned essentially with an understanding of the immigrants' problems faced in this country in the light of their background and aspirations. Research methods included personal interviews (where necessary in the mother tongue), postal questionnaires and participant observation in group activities. A number of individual case histories was built up concerning the respondents' background, education, occupation, household composition, health, social life, mobility, recreation and leisure activities, household possessions, religion and their outlook and attitude towards change experienced in this country. In this way snapshots of the various elements in the immigrant communities, their local problems and their expectancies were prepared.

A number of important conclusions emerged. The report which accompanied this study drew attention to some which have distinct planning relevance.[50] In the first place there was the fairly obvious, but very frequently, neglected observation that there is not one immigrant community but several and 'it is fair to say that the existence and continuance of these separate groups, each with distinctive traditions and values, adds to the general enrichment of society. The real benefit of city life is that an assembly is permitted of the widest possible variety of people representing the strangest minorities of opinions, values, life styles and requirements. The influx of the coloured immigrant adds to the kaleidoscope of city experiences.' The planner's very concept of cities and city life, and his avowed aim of achieving rich and varied exchanges in social intercourse, is pertinent to such observations.

Secondly the study revealed with regard to housing the fact of underprivilege for the majority of the immigrants: low housing standards, and non-accessibility to the widest choice. Allied to this there was the pronounced social status consciousness of the immigrant elite and the strong desire amongst this section to live in middle class areas of the host community. These aspects promote consideration of a very difficult area of housing policy which is highly relevant to social planning, namely the question as to how far one should seek to scatter or concentrate immigrant community areas. More research is needed on what are the housing requirements or aspirations of the majority of the immigrants. On the one hand close kinship networks and tight community groupings give support to members in the face of an alien environment. On the other, it is important to know how far certain characteristics of immigrant life (district concentrations and acceptance of low housing standards in terms of crowding, space and household arrangements, and of multiple occupation) are imposed by local circumstances, and whether, if these constraints were removed, these features might be rejected by forces in emulation of the English middle class. Attitudes are at the present time largely divided on this issue: as policies are more decisively formulated the planner's contribution by way of research and comprehensive environmental concern is required.

Rural Problems

It will be regarded as in no way unusual for rural studies to be considered within the planner's field. The very term 'town and country planning' is of long usage; plans for villages and small towns have been prepared in the same way as for larger urban settlements, and the countryside from the point of view of landscape potential and recreation has always received considerable attention.

But traditionally the planner has tended to consider rural areas, and conceive his proposals towards them, in the light of a static rather than an adaptive approach. For example, plans for rural areas have been prepared essentially in land use terms, as elsewhere. But there are social issues in rural planning just as there are in urban planning, and this accentuates the need for an adaptive outlook.

Some of these issues are of long standing. For example, rural depopulation is likely to continue to present local and regional problems and demand both detailed and broad-based studies. The agricultural parts of the country have lost labour to urban employment since the middle of the nineteenth century, and this drift is almost certain to continue with increased farm mechanization and rationalization of farm holdings. The countryside has rarely been more prosperous, but relatively fewer workers than ever before are required to maintain it. In these circumstances a host of community problems ensue.

In many areas the decline has been such that the rural population is now so small that there are great difficulties in maintaining adequate social services. Except where a distinct hierarchy of rural settlements can be established and larger focal points enhanced as service centres, local authority investment tends to be very thinly spread, with consequent effects on health, education and welfare services. A complementary feature is that there is a marked lack of employment opportunity for women; this contributes to a lower than average total household income, so accenting the disparity between the standards of living of towns and country areas. Further, we might note that although private car ownership rates are usually high in rural areas, a fact which accentuates the problems of maintaining an efficient public transport system, even so a large number of individual journeys are necessary, especially where there are children in the family, and this degree of enforced mobility (in which some, such as the elderly, cannot perhaps share) makes for difficulties in social organization.

The emigrant population is usually of working age, and hence the truly rural areas have an ageing as well as a stable or declining population, a position exacerbated by inward migration from urban areas of retired persons who want to live in rural settlements, possibly returning to their birthplaces. The result is that rural communities frequently have a relatively slender-based age pyramid, weighted towards the middle and upper age brackets, and certain social problems are accentuated. For example, because of their numbers, and because old people most usually depend on fixed incomes, poverty may be widely distributed.

These facts of underprivilege in rural communities mark them out as areas where the deepest understanding of problems is necessary as a prelude to any form of planning intervention. The need for a disproportionate investment of resources, both human and material, to overcome or at least cope with these problems has been recognized for many years. These general points are well known to planning authorities dealing with rural communities. But now there are other aspects relating to changing circumstances in country areas, and these present new issues for the planner.

The actual elements of change in the countryside are many and varied. Agriculture is changing with new, perhaps discordant, elements such as factory farming; and the landscape itself shows new features with buildings in non-traditional materials, hedgerows removed or machine-trimmed to a strange artificiality, and new field patterns. The compactness of village life is changing with greater personal mobility and a wider dependence on centres for work or recreation elsewhere. Moreover, the traditional social structure based on the agricultural labourer, but with the 'establishment' of landed gentry and the church in prominence, has long been in erosion. As Ruth Crichton writes in her study of the Berkshire village of Stratfield Mortimer: 'Today little is left of the old social order. Small businesses are disappearing; large houses have become institutions; the need for local social provision has lessened, and village life is becoming more impersonal as a new, mobile, immigrant population is increasing.'[51]

This last factor of new people coming to live in the country is both a cause and effect of the blurred distinction between the traditional concept of rural and urban worlds, and raises important new questions. Ever since the emergence of a prosperous middle class, dependent on commerce or manufacture, there has been the tendency for people who have acquired wealth in the cities to move out into the countryside, and this characteristic is assuming a new dimension.

In the first place, 'second homes' are now favoured and sought after by a much wider section of society than the very rich. This will almost certainly not have the effect of producing a new era of 'stately homes'; the aim is much more modest, but while the visual effect in terms of building and landscape may be minimal there are a number of important side issues which will be far reaching. The second home movement is of course bound up with demands for recreation and leisure in the countryside and stems from forces such as personal mobility, greater affluence and the result of a more flexible (if not necessarily shorter) working week, all of which permit a number of visits during the year to places perhaps 100 miles or more distant from the home area. If water, either inland or sea, is also available so much the better.

The second home owner becomes temporarily a member of a new community, unless the property is unusually remote. His place may be an ephemeral one, but where a number of second home residents begins to constitute a significant minority of the total population, it would be interesting to record the impact on the host community; it might be assumed that integration would not be easy. One important side effect of the demand for second homes is that while on the one hand there may be some boost to the local economy in the form of demand for services, one unfortunate result is to inflate the prices of houses for sale and so cause unexpected difficulties for local residents.

But numerically and in other ways too, a much more important issue is the substantial change which is taking place in rural areas closest to the larger towns. Urban population is increasing both relatively and absolutely, and moreover the amount of urban land per head of population has dramatically increased in recent years due largely to lower residential densities and higher standards of provision of ancillary land such as schools, playing fields and other open space. Areas devoted to urban development have therefore spread peripherally, limited only by the degree of infilling available in the urban or semi-urban area already covered. There are a number of social forces at work here, but briefly they are concerned with the demand for housing of a particular type and price and in an area which will convey the maximum advantages of status and prestige.

There are two main issues for the planner. One is the characteristics of the new communities themselves, which demand study. The other is the contemporary situation whereby the distinction between urban and rural environments and societies has become much less marked.

The work done by Pahl on a sector of the Greater London fringe in Hertfordshire is very helpful for the planner concerned with these issues.[52] A comprehensive survey was conducted of parishes lying between Hertford, Stevenage and Welwyn Garden City; all the journeys made by all the members of the household outside the parish were recorded and related to various social characteristics. A principal finding was that various groups in the parishes were becoming segregated in their life styles not only as between age, sex and social class characteristics, but also geographically. Houses of a particular type, built in groups, were attracting people with similar economic and social characteristics. This is normal enough, but when grafted on to an established rural settlement the local social status hierarchies are disrupted; the middle class commuter, it is argued, who seeks a meaningful community actually helps to destroy the community which existed.

A distinct new settlement pattern is being forged in rural fringes such as this. Admittedly the outer metropolitan area is extreme in this connection, but the evidence is still relevant for the areas surrounding most larger cities and conurbations. Here, the characteristics of rural settlements, now with their commuter populations, are quite different from anything previously recorded. It may be claimed that these areas no longer have specifically rural problems, but rather regional problems: an urban way of life with urban expectations is now superimposed on a different geographical base. A new diffused residential neighbourhood has been created, the central feature of which is a complex pattern of commuting to a number of central places. This recognition presents the planner with an understanding of the process of the creation of megalopolis or of a loose framework of a city region, and it also poses the need for a new approach to social and physical planning policies at regional scale. By concentrating on land use, only part of the problem is considered: concern for the new social and spatial patterns now emerging should result in radically different planning concepts.

Leisure and Recreation

There has been a growing realization that leisure opportunities will increase substantially for most people in the future, that disposable incomes for spending on recreation will be greater, and that the society of the not-so-distant future will, through education, be keener and perhaps more able to participate in the arts or in sport. These circumstances present a new challenge to the planner. While the planning *of* leisure is an impossible proposition, planning *for* leisure is a method of ensuring that individuals may exercise choice in recreational activities, and as an objective is therefore one of the main elements of social planning.

This is an issue which has been assuming increasingly important proportions during the present decade. The present situation is far from satisfactory: there is lack of co-operation between developers, fragmentation of local authority responsibility and a virtual absence, until recently, of comprehensive regional or sub-regional provision on a properly planned basis. There is accordingly both duplication of efforts and an inadequacy of provision. But in spite of these circumstances (and possibly because of them) the planner has responded well to the challenge of a changing and developing situation which has led to new demands and pressures. This contrasts favourably with the apathy shown towards other aspects of change, say in housing demands or in evolving urban and rural communities. The surprise is even more marked when we note that there are potentially other 'contenders' in the recreational field; the educationalists for example within the local authority system may have conceivably taken the lead. But perhaps because ultimately sites are required for the provision of facilities, perhaps also because there is an element of glamour about leisure and recreation (as opposed say to the understanding of an urban slum) and perhaps because of the co-ordinating work of Regional Sports Councils where the Planning Officer has become a welcome technical adviser—perhaps because of these factors—planners have assumed a professional and technical responsibility.

The potential which leisure time offers to society is tremendous. In former societies leisure for a minority was available through slavery; leisure for the majority might now be forthcoming by reason of the machine. For the first time society can now support a growing leisure class. The contemporary challenge is to exploit the full use of leisure time and recreation so that new pursuits not only become meaningful in developing personal satisfactions but also contribute to a democratizing process of breaking down social barriers and opening up new contacts and shared opportunities.

The planner's task is therefore to facilitate the development of a wide range of leisure outlets which are both personal and purposive. This takes him far away from traditionally conceived concepts of planning for recreation which was seen mainly in land use terms. It extends his interest and concern beyond standards for playing fields or allotments or the provision of facilities such as tennis courts or swimming baths. Instead, he is given the opportunity of developing a new co-ordinating role, with the requirement to provide a comprehensive range of provision from local to district and to regional scale. The distribution of children's play spaces, the development of community centre workshops, a neighbourhood library, a district sports centre, a golf course, a town centre cinema and a regional theatre are instances of the varied components of a comprehensive plan for leisure.

This extension of the planner's horizon presents him with a profitable field of research opportunities. There will be a constant demand for new information and fresh insights on what is motivating individuals and groups in the community to develop their leisure patterns in the way they do. In addition there will be predictive work in the constant process of attempting to forecast demand for a variety of facilities. The extent of this very large field can only be hinted at here, but we might usefully stress the changing social issues in the situations which are of particular relevance.

There are five main factors which the planner has to take into account: rising affluence, an extension of educational opportunity, extended leisure time, increased mobility, and changes in fashion in leisure pursuits. Their significance for the rest of the century has been neatly evaluated by Michael Dower as follows:

	1955	1965	2000 (projected)
Population (millions)	49	52	70
Income (£ per head, 1955 values)	250	325	1,000
Persons over 15 at school and university (thousands)	429	930	2,000
Persons beyond retirement age (millions)	7	8	12
Basic industrial working week (hours)	45	42	30
Cars (millions)	$3\frac{1}{2}$	7	30

Source: Michael Dower, 'Fourth Wave, the challenge of leisure', *The Architects' Journal*, 20 January 1965. Reprinted by the Civic Trust.

Broadly speaking, rising incomes increase the demand for leisure facilities at a compound rate. For example, during the 1950s in Britain a one per cent rise in real income was accompanied by a three per cent increase in real expenditure on annual holidays. There is clearly a willingness to channel 'disposable income' into sport, recreation and leisure generally, and minority pastimes which have had a limited number of adherents on cost grounds are now receiving greater support, demand for facilities increasing accordingly.

With regard to extended educational opportunity, not only are cultural and recreational activities now more accepted in school curricula as part of the education of the 'whole person' in schools, but they are being made available to a greater proportion of the teenage population than ever before. In England and Wales, nearly 20 per cent of young persons aged 15–19 were attending grant-aided schools in 1967, a proportion which will increase, and it is clear that the force of this element of change will be enhanced. Surveys suggest a positive correlation between education and leisure activities, and this increase in 'educational level' should have a marked effect over the whole leisure spectrum from an increased awareness of the arts to increased participation in active recreation pursuits.

Extended leisure time is a further underlying factor in a rapidly changing situation. First, there is the shorter standard working week, and while no great reduction has been achieved in this country since the war, there are forecasts of more significant decreases in the future. Secondly, there is the shorter working year: the Holidays with Pay Act, 1938, provided a fortnight's minimum paid holiday, and this period is gradually being extended. There are other factors also to consider, ranging for example from the impact of the five-day week, to shift working and the question of time spent on journeys to work.

Prediction is difficult in this field, because there are so many alternatives. There is for instance the possibility of a four-day working week compared with the retention of a five-day week and a much longer annual holiday, and the selection of one as opposed to the other would have far-reaching consequences for leisure patterns in society and the provision of facilities at local, regional, national and international levels. As another example of options there is the alternative that instead of seeking more leisure time people may pursue higher financial rewards through primary and/or second jobs ('moonlighting'). Again, the consequences of either in terms of recreational pursuits may be strikingly different.

With regard to increased mobility, the geographical horizons for most people have of course been extended dramatically. This has been the trend for a period of 100 years or more, first by popular train excursions and then by coach, car and air, and the process will continue at an accelerating pace, so that recreational needs may be met many miles from place of residence. As an immediate practical point, the extension of motorways in this country is permitting certain rural areas to be within a new catchment of urban populations: M6 for example has the effect of bringing the Lake District into easy motoring reach of not only South Lancashire but the West Midlands. The car is the great agency of personal and family mobility, and leisure facilities obviously now have to be provided on a regional basis to cater for the very wide range of activities at various scales—weekday, weekend and holiday activities in both urban and rural centres.

Changes in fashion in leisure pursuits are extremely difficult to predict. So far, trends have been estimated from the use of existing facilities over time, but this revealed demand is of course distorted by the existing pattern of supply; we do not really know how consumers might opt for different leisure pursuits if they were available. The rapid rise and fall in popularity of ten-pin bowling is an example of the practical difficulties which arise. But there are underlying social trends which the planner will like to consider; for instance there are the possible changes in working class leisure habits, there is the decline in popularity of certain mass entertainments, and conversely there is the growth in popularity of activities where people compete in relatively small groups, where the sexes meet, where the organizational factor is low and where there might be a considerable age range of active participation. It is necessary to try to anticipate future pressure on facilities, and these are some of the issues involved.

In this field of leisure and recreation the specialist social planner is faced with a formidable array of reading matter. There has been a number of important publications in recent years with which he should be familiar. These include the Study Reports of the Outdoor Recreation Resources Review Commission (ORRRC)[53] which describe the American situation, and the British Travel Association/University of Keele report on their national recreation survey in this country.[54] There is in fact now a good deal of literature, both American and British, and this is expanding rapidly; a useful bibliography has been prepared by Palmer[55] and this indicates the range of the specialist body of knowledge which is now being accumulated.

REFERENCES TO CHAPTER 3

1. Octavia Hill, 'Homes of the London Poor', *Macmillan's Magazine*, October 1871, quoted in *Octavia Hill*, E. Moberley Bell, Constable, 1946.

2. Jane Jacobs, *The Death and Life of Great American Cities*, Jonathan Cape, 1962.
3. Donald L. Foley, in *Explorations into Urban Structure*, University of Pennsylvania Press, 1964.
4. Melvin M. Webber, *Order in Diversity: Community without Propinquity*, in *Cities in Space*, editor Lowdon Wingo, Johns Hopkins, 1963.
5. Homer Hoyt, 'Growth and Structure of Twenty One Great World Cities', *Land Economics*, Vol. XLII, No. 1, February 1966.
6. Louis Wirth, 'Urbanism as a Way of Life', *The American Journal of Sociology*, Vol. XLIV, No. 1, July 1938.
7. F. Stuart Chapin and Shirley F. Weiss (editors), *Urban Growth Dynamics in a Regional Cluster of Cities*, John Wiley, 1962.
8. Leonard Reissman, *The Urban Process: Cities in Industrial Societies*, The Free Press of Glencoe, 1964.
9. Charles Frankel, *The Family in Context*, in *Helping the Family in Urban Society*, editor Fred Delliquadri, Columbia University Press, 1963.
10. C. Rosser and C. Harris, *The Family and Social Change; a study of family and kinship in a South Wales town*, Routledge, 1965.
11. James Kirkup, *Sorrows, Passions and Alarms*, Collins, 1959.
12. Richard Hoggart, *The Uses of Literacy*, 1957, quoted in John Madge, 'Privacy and Social Interaction', *Transactions of the Bartlett Society*, Vol. 3, 1964–5.
13. J. R. Seeley, *Crestwood Heights*, New York, 1956, quoted in John Madge 'Privacy and Social Interaction', *Transactions of the Bartlett Society*, Vol. 3, 1964–5.
14. H. J. Gans, *The Levittowners; ways of life and politics in a new suburban community*, Allen Lane, 1967.
15. John H. Goldthorpe, David Lockwood, Frank Bechhoffer and Jennifer Platt, 'The Affluent Worker and the Thesis of Embourgeoisement', *Sociology*, Vol. 1, No. 1, January 1967.
16. N. Elias and J. L. Scotson, *The Established and the Outsiders*, Frank Cass, 1965.
17. R. N. Morris and John Mogey, *Studies at Berinsfield*, Routledge, 1965.
18. H. E. Bracey, *Neighbours on New Estates and Subdivisions in England and U.S.A.*, Routledge, 1964.
19. Peter Hall, *London 2000*, Faber & Faber, 1963.
20. D. A. Reeder, 'A Theatre of Suburbs: Some Patterns of Development in West London, 1801–1911', in *The Study of Urban History*, editor H. J. Dyos, Edward Arnold, 1968.
21. Larry A. Sjaastad, 'The Costs and Returns of Human Migration', *Journal of Political Economy*, Vol. 70, No. 5, Part 2, October 1962.
22. P. H. Rossi, *Why Families Move; a study in the social psychology of urban residential mobility*, The Free Press of Glencoe, 1955.
23. *Mobility and the North*, Technical Committee of Planning Officers, North Regional Planning Committee, July 1967.
24. F. Musgrove, *The Migratory Elite*, Heinemann, 1963.

25. Marc Fried, *Grieving For a Lost Home*, in *The Urban Condition*, editor Leonard J. Duhl, Basic Books, 1964.
26. Norman S. Power, *The Forgotten People*, Arthur James, 1965.
27. Gordon E. Cherry, 'Overcrowding in Cities', *Official Architecture and Planning*, Vol. 32, No. 3, March 1969.
28. John B. Calhoun, 'Population Density and Social Pathology', *Scientific American*, February 1962.
29. James Plant, *The Personality and an Urban Area*, in *Cities and Society*, editors P. K. Hatt and A. J. Reiss, The Free Press of Glencoe, 1957.
30. Peter Sainsbury, *Suicide in London: an ecological study*, The Institute of Psychiatry, 1955.
31. A. F. Philp, *Family Failure*, Faber & Faber, 1963.
32. Gordon E. Cherry, *Social Malaise and the Environment*, British Association, Leeds, 1967.
33. R. M. Titmuss in *Growing up in the City; a study of juvenile delinquency in an urban neighbourhood*, J. B. Mays, Liverpool University Press, 1956.
34. I. M. Castle and E. Gittus, 'The Distribution of Social Defects in Liverpool', *The Sociological Review*, Vol. 5, No. 1, July 1957.
35. Peter Scott, 'Delinquency, Mobility and Broken Homes in Hobart', *Australian Journal of Social Issues*, Vol. 2, 1965.
36. C. Bagley, 'Juvenile Delinquency in Exeter, an Ecological and Comparative Study', *Urban Studies*, Vol. 2, No. 1, May 1965.
37. I. M. Castle and E. Gittus, *op. cit.*
38. J. Spencer, *Stress and Release in an Urban Estate*, Tavistock Publications, 1964.
39. Gordon E. Cherry, *op. cit.*
40. Lord Taylor and Sidney Chave, *Mental Health and Environment*, Longmans, 1964.
41. E. H. Hare and G. K. Shaw, *Mental Health on a New Housing Estate*, Oxford University Press, 1965.
42. D. W. K. Kay, P. Beamish and Martin Roth, 'Old Age Mental Disorders in Newcastle upon Tyne', *The British Journal of Psychiatry*, Vol. 110, No. 468, September 1964.
43. Erwin Stengel, *Suicide and Attempted Suicide*, Penguin, 1964.
44. *Report of Working Party on Problem Families*. Joint Sub-Committee as to Rehabilitation, City and County of Newcastle upon Tyne, January 1966.
45. A. F. Philp, *op. cit.*
46. Peter Marris and Martin Reid, *Dilemmas of Social Reform*, Routledge, 1967.
47. B. Abel-Smith and P. Townsend, *The Poor and the Poorest; a new analysis of the Ministry of Labour's Family Expenditure Survey of 1953–54 and 1960*, G. Bell, 1965.
48. K. Coates and Richard Silburn (Editors), *The Morale of the Poor; a survey of poverty on a Nottingham council estate*, Department of Adult Education, Nottingham University, 1968.
49. Hannah H. Meissner (editor), *Poverty in the Affluent Society*, Harper & Row, 1966.

50. W. Burns, *The Coloured Immigrant in Newcastle upon Tyne*, City and County of Newcastle upon Tyne, October 1967.
51. Ruth Crichton, *Commuters' Village*, David T. Charles, 1964.
52. R. E. Pahl, *Urbs in Rure—the Metropolitan Fringe in Hertfordshire*, London School of Economics and Political Science, Geographical Papers No. 2, 1965.
53. Study Reports, Outdoor Recreation Resources Review Commission, U.S. Government Printing Office, 1962.
54. British Travel Association/University of Keele, *Pilot National Recreation Survey: Report No. 1*, British Travel Association, 1967.*
55. J. E. Palmer, 'Recreational Planning—a Bibliographical Review', *Planning Outlook*, Vol. 2, Spring 1967.

* Now supplemented by *Report No. 2*, 1969. See also K. K. Sillitoe, *Planning for Leisure*, Government Social Survey, H.M.S.O., 1969.

4

A Framework for Social Planning Policies

In postulating a framework for social planning policies, it is first of all necessary to consider the underlying philosophy and social objectives of planning itself and the assumptions on which these are based. Planners have been somewhat diffident about laying bare the bones of their ideologies, and, as a result, a tightly argued body of planning theory has been but poorly defined. A notable contribution has however been made by Foley, with the argument that three substantive propositions state the main ideologies.[1] Let us examine these in turn.

Firstly, Foley considers that planning's main task is to reconcile competing claims for the use of limited land in order to provide a consistent, balanced and orderly arrangement of land uses. There can be little doubt that this task has been planning's most recognizable and successful function in post-war years. The development plan and its periodic review has been an accepted part of the statutory planning system, and the new emphasis on urban structure helps to consolidate this area of work in which the planner has so many technical skills to contribute.

Secondly, Foley's premise is that the function of planning is to provide a good or better physical environment. This goes beyond the first objective which, as an allocating function, is neutral; instead, there is something to champion. But there is a sting in the tail. 'Either town planning conceives of this physical environment as sufficiently an end in itself, as a quality to be strived for, while the social-spatial patterns of urban living work themselves out through other mechanisms than town planning. . . . Or town planning openly accepts the better physical environment as merely an intermediate goal, in which case the critical question must also be asked: intermediate to what further social goals?'

It is certainly true that planning has fought strongly to secure 'improvement to environment' both in development projects and in the last twenty years through the statutory control of development. The history of planning control during these two decades does not lack for evidence of concern for the environment: conditions may be attached to planning permissions such as 'in order to safeguard (or enhance) the amenities of the area' and planning permission refused on the grounds of 'detriment to amenity'. It may well be questioned however why there is so much concern about improvements to the physical environment when it seems to make relatively little difference to the people who are most affected.

Perhaps the emphasis on a rational external order of things is simply a reflection of a creative self-expression which sees the control of development (in the planning sense) as an act of art in the building of landscape. This may be so, especially in town building exercises in civic design terms, but it is still the case that many efforts to manipulate the physical environment have a purposive view in mind, not just to provide aesthetic satisfaction but to influence behaviour in the widest sense. It is strange that this aim has been pursued so long; as we have seen, the evidence that supports physical environment determinism is both tentative and complex.

We have argued in Chapter 2 that the social goals of planning are only partially met by a concern for the physical environment. At the heart of the matter must lie a question of attitudes: social planning is either a matter of social *evolution* or social *engineering*. Planners by tradition have seen their role as community builders and shapers of society. We now argue that social planning strategy is concerned more with the promotion of satisfaction through the provision of a range of opportunity and choice so that the unhampered creativity of individuals may be fostered. This means that social planning objectives are to limit as far as possible those social, physical and economic constraints which operate in the environment and in the institutional framework in such a way as to preclude individuals or groups from fully experiencing or sharing in the conditions for maximum happiness.

Foley's third point is that as part of a broader social programme, town planning provides the physical basis for better urban community life, with ideals such as (a) the provision of low-density residential areas, (b) the fostering of local community life and (c) the control of conurban growth. Foley was writing in 1960, and these examples now look rather dated. Consistent falls in urban densities have been recorded from the Census data of 1951, 1961 and 1966 and the adverse social consequences of high-density living have now lost some of their force; indeed, multi-occupation within a dwelling may be a much more serious problem locally than the fact of sheer density over a given area. Again, 'local community life' is not regarded with the same importance because a more extensive pattern of individual contacts is tending to limit the role of the local community as a support-giving institution and as a medium for inculcating local pride and community consciousness. As far as conurban growth is concerned, there are also signs of changing attitudes. The obsession with constraints on urban growth by the promotion of satellite communities has characterized British planning so far, but in recent years examples such as proposals for large cities in South Hampshire or for corridor-sector development in the South-East have indicated a readiness to think of new cities and city regions of different forms with revised ideas on size and structure.

Foley is right to stress planning's role in providing the physical basis for urban community life, but we might now widen his proposition. We have argued that social planning is a process primarily concerned with extending opportunities and opening up choices for people. Because the greater part of our society is urban, these opportunities and choices are to be provided largely in urban areas; the nature of the urban environment and our attitude to large cities in particular is therefore critical.

An anti-urban tradition is very influential, and the instinctive reaction on the part of many people is to hold at arm's length the spectre of the ever-increasing size of cities. To quote Foley again: 'Running throughout the British social ideology of cities . . . is the distinct and strong suspicion that great cities do not provide really decent living places for the bulk of their populations.'[2] This feeling is manifest in a number of ways, not least in literary evidence which suggests the city of the future as intolerable. For example, H. G. Wells's *Time Machine* (1894) conceived this city consisting of an Upper World of ruins and an Under World in the bowels of the earth where people lived permanently underground. Anatole France's *Penguin Island* (1909) presented a city covered by smoke so that its people (15 million) had to breathe artificial air.

Perhaps it is the seemingly remorseless inevitability of large city growth which is perturbing. Doxiadis had expressed this growth graphically in respect of Athens where 'seven people, three cars and four dwellings are added every hour, and three square feet of area every second',[3] with the result that the city which for 3,000 years had a population of less than 50,000 has in the last century jumped to 2,500,000.

The other disturbing aspect to which attention is drawn is the capacity of cities to accommodate and intensify so many unsatisfactory features of life. The anti-urbanist points to delinquency and crime, to the slums and the segregated populations, and concludes that sheer size makes for unmanageability. He further points to the large sections of city populations who are effectively excluded from many city activities and who lack the opportunity to participate in city life; on the other hand it is claimed that relatively more inhabitants of the small town can share in a wider sphere of activities. In the end, the city as a living unit is deserted for suburb, and for Margaret Mead at any rate this is 'the most atrocious ekistical invention made in the history of the human race' where 'people are segregated by age, by income, by ethnic group, by religion, and by a series of other wearisome temperamental characteristics'.[4]

In contrast, those who do not share these views point to the tremendous vitality of cities and the heterogeneity which brings together a diverse profusion of the characteristics of human life. In the words of Walt Whitman,

> This is the city and I am one of the citizens,
> Whatever interests the rest interests me, politics, wars,
>   markets, newspapers, schools,
> The mayor and councils, banks, tariffs, steamships,
>   factories, stocks, stores, real estate and personal
>   estate.[5]

In large cities lie the seeds of greater human satisfaction than ever before; the potentials are recognized, but the danger is also exposed, and this is the challenge for the social planner.

There are a number of recognizable forces which suggest that big cities will continue to grow and that megalopolis now identified in embryo in America and also in Western Europe, is inevitable. But it would be unwise at this stage to overemphasize this trend. Megalopolis is the experience of a very short period of time and it is difficult to claim that it is an inevitable evolutionary process. But even so, there is an urgent task to examine the consequences of this new phenomenon of city size and the loose spatial arrangement of city regions. On the one hand sheer size may maximize efficiency and variety and provide for human contact and communication in a world of increased personal mobility and rapid social change, but on the other hand it may contribute to congestion and social disorganization.

In considering urban size we should remember that there is not one environment, but many: for example the biochemical, the physical, the psychological and the socio-cultural. There are therefore different kinds of environmental stresses. In the industrial cities of the nineteenth century the chief dangers were forthcoming in industrial safety and public health. Today these have largely been eliminated in the western world, but new adverse urban by-products have emerged. Cities, transport, and the working environment all place a number of stresses on the human physical organism. We are led to believe that the impact of certain artifacts and densities are particularly harmful to man, but the difficulty is that a large share of behavioural science must be interpreted by analogy (for example the experiments on rats and mice, as we have seen). Planners have been more concerned with density than scale and size, but the effects of the latter are now as important to measure as the former. There should be a fruitful research field in tracing the environmental implications of urban complexes.

It is important to see the city as a social mechanism for sustaining human contact. In the belief that intimate contacts are essential for human survival and that each person requires not one but several intimate contacts at any given time, it is necessary for the future city to continue to provide this facility. At the present time the traditional mechanism of the primary groups, which sustain a high level of intimate contacts, is weakening, and in some extreme localized cases may be said to have broken down. With the growing significance of secondary groups as opposed to primary groups, the total number of contacts may have increased but these with any one person become shorter, less frequent and less meaningful from the human point of view. The vestige of the primary group remains of course in the family but with household fission the number of adults remaining with intimate contact may be just two, with a substantial minority only one.

Alexander has argued that people need three or four intimate contacts at every moment of their lives in order to survive; without these they undergo 'progressive deterioration and disintegration'.[6]

One consequence of urbanization is that individuals may be auto-
nomous, and able to exist independently. As Alexander remarks,
'Women can make a living on their own; teenagers no longer
need their families; old people can fend for themselves; men are
able to get meals from the local automat, or from the freezer in
the supermarket.'

We have argued previously that urban man now belongs much
less to one inclusive community; in a multi-group society his social
interests become specialized and part (but rarely all) of the
allegiance formerly given to local communities may be transferred
to specific interest groups. This trend in society away from ascrip-
tive status in self-contained groups towards a much more fluid
grouping in which a man's position is due to competition and
contract, and in which the groups to which he belongs are not
exclusive, is of course of long standing. Sharp historical distinc-
tions may be seen. To quote Mason: 'In the Middle Ages if you
belonged to the Guild of Tanners you probably had few social
links outside it; your commitment to a Highland clan before 1745
was still more sharply overriding. Today, in a typically middle
class setting, you might belong to the Society of Chartered
Accountants as well as a church congregation, a tennis club or
bird-watching association, a political party, an amateur dramatic
group.'[7]

In present-day society both the familistic and the spatial groups
have weakened and the urbanite is increasingly attached to a series
of special interest groups for support and social needs rather than
the family or the neighbourhood. In these circumstances can we
be optimistic about the city and its capacity for accommodating
a meaningful urban way of life in human terms?

There are two extreme approaches to this problem. On the one
hand we may conclude that the necessary intimate contact can
only be substained adequately by primary groups in a spatial
system, as in the past. This would induce us to maintain the *status
quo* in the form and shape of British cities, to resist the forces of
change which are encouraging their growth and to resist above
all the trend towards cities of extreme size.

On the other hand we may come to the conclusion that adult
primary groups have had their day, that it is unrealistic either
to try to recreate them or to sustain them in the future society,
and that the physical structure of the city of the future need not
be concerned about them. Hence a new social mechanism would
be needed to sustain the necessary level of intimate, informal daily

contact between people without the traditional support of the primary group.

The planner may well feel bewildered at having to consider these options, concluding that he has neither the ability, nor should he have the responsibility, for either crystal-gazing or taking decisions on such fundamental questions. Yet the intellectual challenge has to be faced if he is to show that by reason of his technical skills and comprehensive grasp of essentials he has a voice to be reckoned with in contributing to the evolving form of urban society. This is the time for the planner to come of age and for him fully to recognize the social context of his work.

In considering the urban dilemma extreme situations have been deliberately posed. By and large, British towns and cities have not exploded spatially in the way that American counterparts have done, and the evidence of changing social systems in a wider urban environment is localized. The degree of change is still limited. From the physical point of view at least, just as most of our towns and cities are still Victorian, so in fifty years' time they will still very probably retain the character and form of the mid-twentieth century. In Britain there is an established pattern of urban development, spatially throughout the country as a whole, and an established character internally within the urban areas themselves. Although forces of change are apparent, their relative effect will be to realign and redirect rather than overthrow present-day characteristics.

From the social point of view the world of most people is still highly localized and there are many who need local community contacts; there is of course a whole range of normal, average families, but in particular there are people such as the aged, or the handicapped in one form or another who need the supports which a neighbourhood and community can give. It is misleading to overemphasize the psychological mobility of urban man and his weaker ties with a particular neighbourhood or his own parental family. These ties are by no means non-existent; families exist and for most people they involve their members in inescapable relationships. Therefore each neighbourhood has its own cohesion and there is still a high degree of social intercourse centred on contact between neighbours, the special world of children, daily shopping and so on. This enables us to plan or provide for an overlapping system of neighbour, community and special interest group, thus retaining the contemporary basis, but allowing for new forces to be manifest where required. This will allow for regional differences within this country whereby some city regions will remain more 'traditional' than others.

So we may conclude that the ideal of an intimate and cohesive form of social living remains valid, and still to a large extent we can realistically think of geographically based units of organization. We shall consider the question of the neighbourhood in later pages but we can observe now that there is still qualified merit in an urban form which provides for local communities with personal relationships based on sustained ties with neighbours with or without the extended family. It is all a question of degree. For some communities in certain areas this basis will be particularly relevant; for others elsewhere the needs of a new pluralistic social structure, organized into collateral systems, will be much more pronounced and it will be necessary to accept an identification with wide, non-local, special interest groups. There will be the need to experiment with a number of mechanisms in order to provide for an optimum level of human contact; there will be spatial groups and special-interest groups, and towns of different size and structure in different locations will demand the most careful monitoring of requirements and the evaluation of current trends. The value of adaptive as opposed to static planning approaches will be readily apparent.

In drawing together the threads of this examination we might note that there has been the tendency to assume that land use and technological variables were the 'givens' in city planning and the forms of community life or the institutions were the 'takens'. This can no longer be so. Human values, norms and beliefs all make a difference in shaping social structure, political processes, economic development, technology and even land use patterns. Physical planning can have no meaningful basis without a full recognition of the requirements of the community; to this extent the contribution of the specialist social planner is an inescapable part of the total planning process. One can conceive technological solutions for a city plan: it is necessary that these fit and harmonize as closely as possible with community requirements, changing as they are because of a range of forces and pressures. We have argued that the fundamental concern must be to provide for an optimum level of human contact, and that in the British context, this means a basis of recognizing the value of the primary group in localized communities but also allowing for wider social systems on an increasing scale. Constant monitoring of change during the coming years will suggest the pace of adaption that will be necessary, but at this stage it would be unrealistic to think that massive shifts of emphasis were likely to take place in anything like the immediate future.

Beyond this, we have concluded that the planner's accustomed role of manipulation of the physical environment in order to secure 'improvement' is a perfectly viable objective. But the aim is not however to influence behaviour or to achieve certain desiderata in society; rather is it to provide opportunity and choice so that in the process of 'improvement' a variety of environmental settings are provided for the development of human creativity and for full participation in community life.

These considerations allow us to postulate a framework for social planning policies. The traditional functions of social welfare were designed to give support particularly to the weakest members. More recently the emphasis has shifted from supporting the weak and needy, by specific action in respect of them, to public policy as a whole, whereby a process of redistribution of income gives support where it is required. This is analogous to the history of social planning policies. Early social planning objectives were concentrated on the weakest members, for example in improving the living conditions of the working classes, and it would be conceivable on this basis to define a range of individual policies according to selected criteria of need. But we must now go beyond this to a concern for redistribution—not of income but of opportunity. Accordingly, social planning policies should be geared to the provision of opportunity and choice in order to promote the greatest level of satisfaction in society. In this way the expectation would be that the lot of the traditionally weaker or under-privileged members would be strengthened as constraints in the social, physical and economic environments were progressively reduced. There will of course always be certain categories and areas of disadvantage remaining unaffected by these measures, and therefore complementary selective support will be necessary.

Social planning policies will operate at a number of different levels. Some will be designed to help individuals or families on a personal scale, and others to operate impersonally through a small community or in a neighbourhood; some will be designed to redistribute privilege and opportunity and so effect structural changes throughout society.

With this approach we may suggest that social planning policies may be reviewed under the headings shown overleaf.

1. National and regional policies.
2. Community planning at the neighbourhood level.
3. Housing policies.
4. Policies regarding urban renewal.
5. Individual problem groups, such as the immigrant or the delinquent.
6. Social administration.
7. Leisure and recreation.

National and Regional Policies

Recent years have witnessed the revival of interest in regional planning. A proliferation of regional studies has appeared in the last few years and perhaps we are better informed than ever before, even though still superficially, about the character and problems of regions in the country. Additionally, more and more effort is being put into co-ordinating local planning authority objectives in the interests of overall regional strategies.

At the physical level the reasons for regional planning are fairly obvious. In a geographically defined area, especially where there is some 'consciousness' or affinity of interest perhaps centred round the influence of a regional capital or a common employment base, it is clearly beneficial at least to co-ordinate the individual policies of component parts for the benefit of the whole. So far this allocating function has been the main aspect of planning, but we might now go further and see social factors in regional planning objectives.

We can illustrate this social context with reference to two regions of very different character in this country. The terms 'favoured' and 'unfavoured' have been used to summarize regional characteristics on the basis of employment potential and capacity for growth. The favoured regions are usually taken to include the following: East Anglia, South-East, West Midlands, East Midlands and South-West (the latter assuming a very borderline position). Unfavoured regions include Northern, North-West, Wales, Scotland, and East and West Ridings (the latter again assuming borderline characteristics). The examples we shall take are first of all the Northern Region and secondly the West Midlands.

In the Northern Region the most dramatic response to a generally disadvantaged situation has been out-migration at a high level consistently for a number of decades. The Region exports population at a net rate of about 10,000 persons each year, and the out-migrants tend to be the young (0–15 and 30–39 age groups) and the upwardly mobile (in status group terms, the managers and foremen). The reason for this out-movement is undoubtedly associated with a desire for betterment and security in terms of employment and higher wages.[8]

Economically, the Region is severely disadvantaged. With regard to industry and employment the Region has an obsolete industrial base with undue concentrations on coal mining, iron and steel, heavy engineering and shipbuilding, and it has proved unable to widen this base adequately or quickly enough. As a result, activity rates (the proportion of the population of working age actually in the labour force) are low and unemployment rates are high, usually twice the national average, with pockets of chronic unemployment in particular parts. Moreover the duration of unemployment is correspondingly longer. As far as earnings and hours worked are concerned, manual workers in certain manufacturing and other industries have a shorter working week and earn less than elsewhere.

But in other factors, too, the Region has environmental deficiencies.[9] Concerning housing for example, household size is above average, and the average number of rooms per dwelling is lower than anywhere in the country except Scotland. There is a high proportion of pre-1914 dwellings and the Region has the lowest proportion of owner-occupiers apart from Scotland.

From the point of view of education, local education pupils in the Northern Region form a larger proportion of the total number than anywhere else in the country except Wales and Scotland; proportions of pupils in private schools are low. Together with Scotland the region has the highest proportion of pupils leaving at fifteen years, and the region has fewer boys going to universities and colleges than anywhere else.

With regard to health, a key factor is that unfavoured regions generally have more prescriptions per person and higher costs per prescription than the national average. But yet these regions generally have more patients than elsewhere on doctors' lists of over 2,500. On the other hand, a pertinent comparison is that the London and South-East Region has the highest proportion of consultants holding distinction awards.

Social characteristics are pronounced. The Northern Region has a smaller proportion of employers, managers and professional workers than any other region in England and Wales. Average household income is lower than anywhere else in Great Britain.

Family expenditure is relatively low on housing, fuel, light and power, transport and services, but proportionately more than the national average is spent on alcoholic drink and tobacco. As a reflection of the low regional income capacity, the Region in recent years has had amongst the lowest savings in the whole country; the lowest average amount in wills is left here. A further indication is the low car ownership rates.

Similar socio-economic criteria can be offered for other regions, and certainly for parts of Scotland such as the Highlands and Islands, or for Northern Ireland a more adverse picture could be painted. But for the Northern Region and its three-and-a half million people this statistical evaluation highlights the short-comings of five counties which contribute so much to the image of disadvantage presented by the North in general. The factors quoted have been deliberately selective and many favourable aspects have been ignored. The Region has its natural beauty, for example in its hills, rivers and expansive beaches and in its towns as at Durham. It is fair to say too that the Region is changing: Holford's Team Valley Industrial Estate was the first new chal-lenge to depressed areas in the country in the 1930s, and this has been followed by development and redevelopment in many quarters.

But the traditions of the Region die hard: its spoil heaps, quarries and industrial waste, its bare towns ribbed by terraces of inadequate housing, its poverty of environment and a landscape witness to an industrial structure of coal, steel, ships and chemicals are still all too typical. The key is its retardation and a twentieth-century failure to respond to new economic stimuli. Social attitudes, forged by an often bitter employment history, are per-petuated by a realization that opportunity is less and expectations are lower than most other places in the country.

Economic deprivation leads to social deprivation. In an area where there are insufficient jobs, where new employment is not being created fast enough, where there is a lack of labour variety, where opportunities for school leavers are limited, and where insufficient money is being earned under circumstances of irregu-larity and uncertainty, the economic conditions for widely based social satisfaction throughout the community are restricted. These major constraints on the attainment of happiness operate through shortcomings of the social and economic environment; in par-ticular the institutional conditions governing employment are in need of considerable improvement. There is a wide variety of other constraints also: insufficient choice in housing, with considerable room for improvement in the existing dwelling stock, and so on.

A major reason for pursuing regional planning objectives in the Northern Region is therefore not only to co-ordinate internal regional policies or to prepare a regional master plan in land use terms, but also to meet the socio-economic deficiencies which have been outlined. Tackling the employment sources would have a chain reaction which could only be beneficial. Social considerations therefore lie intertwined amid the physical and economic objectives of regional planning; as far as the Northern Region is concerned, these considerations colour the requirement to make the area a better place to live in and to bring satisfaction to the lives of its inhabitants.

The West Midlands by comparison have regional characteristics of rather a different kind. The region has been described as follows:

'Fairly near to the national average in most things and with many social attributes of the industrial north as well as of the south; incomes per head rather above the national average and household incomes quite markedly so; relatively low national assistance payments, but also relatively few personal incomes beyond £1,500; higher than average household spending on most things and in particular on cars and food, but lower than average spending on services; lower than average rates of drunkenness, indictable offences, suicides, and children in care; lower than average proportions of children staying on at school or getting university awards, along with higher than average enrolments in sandwich, part-time and evening courses; bigger than average lists per family doctor and dentist, and less than average spent on prescriptions, fewer than average absences from work for sickness or injury, and few people in employers' sick-pay schemes; fewer than average hospital births and higher than average maternal death rates and perinatal mortality.'[10]

This series of social snapshots presents the West Midlands in a rather different light from the Northern Region. But while there may be a different order of underlying social issues, it is equally important in this region that in the preparation of regional planning policies social aspects are recognized in the evaluation of alternative strategies.

We might develop this from the point of view of economic

growth. One of the key characteristics of the West Midlands is its vigorous expansion of employment, and this of course has social implications of great magnitude. The region has been showing a faster expansion in population than any other region in the country and there is a consequent pressure for accommodation of people and work in and around the principal urban centres. It has been estimated that a sustained regional rate of house-building of around 35,000 dwellings annually will be required to 1981 (630,000 new houses between 1963 and 1981) to remedy existing housing shortages, to replace slums and sub-standard houses and to meet the additional housing needs of a growing population. Of the total, no fewer than 355,000 dwellings will be required for the needs arising from the Birmingham conurbation alone.[11]

A regional strategy for growth, to accommodate the demands for urban development within conceived spatial patterns, can be prepared from a number of alternatives. The heart of the problem is the Birmingham conurbation. First there is the possibility of extending the periphery of the urban core outwards into the surrounding countryside; alternatively the growth might be taken up either by satellite development beyond the green belt, or by the establishment of new independent centres away from the conurbation's sphere of influence, or by the fostering of new areas of development in the form of corridors of growth.

At the present time, overall planning policy for the West Midlands rests on a policy of containment of the conurbation in favour of satellite development beyond a green belt. To this extent there is Redditch and Telford (formerly Dawley) New Towns, and expanded towns such as Tamworth and Daventry. At the same time there has been compromise by virtue of major peripheral development of the conurbation as at Chelmsley Wood in Warwickshire.

Execution of the strategy is meeting with difficulty, because to be properly effective residential displacement to satellites should be accompanied by a commensurate amount of industrial movement if reasonable self-sufficiency is to be achieved. In practice it has been found possible to secure some very extensive population movements in both the public and private sectors, but by comparison the scale of industrial movement, for a variety of reasons, has been slender. Moreover there are inherent factors which suggest that it might never be possible to attain a workable balance of residential movement and job opportunity. Consequently there are a host of social issues surrounding this aspect of regional strategy: for example the divorce of work place and residence, the lack of locally based employment opportunities for female workers and school leavers, and the costs and social acceptability of commuting.

Quite apart from the difficulty of reconciling differential success as between residential and industrial redistribution, the whole question of the evolution of urban form through a conscious regional strategy has a large number of social implications. The consequences of manipulating the physical structure of a complex urban system are very wide, and the social repercussions at least are bound up with the question of housing provision.

There are a number of relevant factors to consider here. There is the question of housing need, as a function of demographic trends and the replacement of unfit dwellings. This is different from housing demand, a product of trends in household income and expenditure and changing densities of occupation. On the other hand there is the question of housing supply: the nature of the housing stock, its adequacy and social acceptability in a period of rapidly rising standards, costs in housing (rents and mortgages), and the operation of private and public authority housing schemes.

Over a wide urban area there is a close relationship between these factors of need, demand and supply. This is manifested in the pattern of residential mobility which occurs, and wide research fields surround the questions 'who moves where, when and why?' In this movement there are 'pushes' and 'pulls' whereby assumed or real inadequacies of living in older, inner urban areas are matched against attractions of new residential areas in the light of rising incomes and aspirations. In addition to the work-place element in spatial strategy it is apparent therefore that the dynamics of city-regional change have both social causes and consequences. The process is concerned with social systems as well as housing systems, and any regional strategy can only be evaluated in the light of a most sophisticated appraisal of the factors surrounding effective housing demand, and opportunities, choice and satisfaction in alternative environments.

Neighbourhood Planning

There has been an enormous shift by the planner in his attitude towards the neighbourhood. A span of only forty years covers the period from the early ideas of Perry, the endorsement of theory by the protagonists of the 1940s, 'textbook' development in the 1950s to disillusionment and a rapid weakening of enthusiasm in the 1960s. Lip service is still paid to the concept in physical design terms, but few prefer now to speak about the sociological implications; to all intents and purposes the idea of neighbourhood as formerly conceived is dead.

It is very instructive to refer back to major planning works of a quarter of a century ago to appreciate the dogma which was then prevalent about community planning. For example, Forshaw and Abercrombie in the *County of London Plan* (1943) declared that 'Community grouping helps in no small measure towards the inculcation of local pride, it facilitates control and organization, and is the means of resolving what would otherwise be interminable aggregations of housing.'[12] The proposal was therefore 'to emphasize the identity of the existing communities, to increase their degree of segregation, and where necessary to reorganize them as separate and definite entities. The aim would be to provide each community with its own schools, public buildings, shops, open spaces, etc.' This organization, it will be recalled, was to be based on 'the desirable scholar-capacity of the elementary school and the desirability of fixing a maximum walking distance from home to school'.

These views represented the high watermark of neighbourhood planning theory. They were taken from London and expressed again in virtually every town and city plan in the country. Nicholas in the *City of Manchester Plan* (1945) for example wrote with even more conviction that 'The function of the neighbourhood is to supply the immediate needs of everyday living. The more self-contained its structure, the greater will be its power to induce a sense of local patriotism and an interest in community life.'[13]

Nicholas's assumptions were:

The intimate social life of the village and small town engenders a natural feeling of community. Everyone knows his neighbours' troubles, feels that their welfare is his own concern, and can freely take his part in the discussion and adoption of collective remedies for common ills. So it was also in the original townships that grew up within the present boundaries of Manchester. But when these separate units coalesced and were absorbed into a sprawling, shapeless mass of bricks and mortar their identity became blurred, and with it the civic sense of their inhabitants. The community became a remote abstraction rather than a fact of everyday experience, the individual could no longer make his voice heard by the vast multitudes of his neighbours, and the means no longer existed whereby a local opinion might crystallize and find effective expression. Manchester, in short, had lost touch with its citizens; it is hardly surprising, then, that most of them lost interest in the growth and government of Manchester. They will relapse into the same isolation after the war if their re-awakened sense of community fails to find a peacetime outlet. It must surely be a primary objective of any plan for Manchester to create a civic structure that will nourish that community feeling and give it scope for truly democratic self-expression.

We have already written at length about the reduction of personal relationships in the local community and the relative increase in contacts in wider society. We have however exercised caution in not over-exaggerating these trends. For large numbers of people, local residential districts still form the immediate known world which gives support through its familiarity, and in which close human contact is developed.

In these circumstances the physical neighbourhood framework is still likely to offer a useful basis for the planning of residential areas. There will however be a number of differences. For example while the framework for the provision of local facilities in the form of schools and services will still be very important, it will not be assumed that neighbourhood self-containment in other directions is necessarily of great value. Additionally, the objective of spatial organization on a neighbourhood basis will no longer be specifically to inculcate community feeling, although this is not to say that local consciousness derived from awareness of a particular environment is not valuable whenever it emerges.

Instead, a main objective will be purely functional: in the internal structure of any urban area there will be developed, as interstices within the ribs of a highway framework, residential areas which by their form, shape, size, history and sense of identity assume a certain homogeneity of character as a neighbourhood. Within this area it will be sensible to provide for local needs, educational, shopping, services and so on.

A related objective is also functional in that it will facilitate the internal physical structuring of the neighbourhood. The small-scale environmental unit as advocated by Buchanan for traffic management purposes might well offer a meaningful local basis for the planning of residential areas. These are on a sufficiently small scale to foster locally based social cohesion where required, but large and loose enough not to inhibit the development of wider interests if this is demanded.

With this basis, the neighbourhood, comprising a number of environmental units, provides a useful rationality in territorial organization. Personal relationships within spatial groups based on sustained ties with neighbours are catered for, while the additional stratum of wider contact is recognized and allowed for. In other words, the new emphasis is on the functionability of the framework and the permissiveness of the internal structure in allowing for the self-expression of small groups; this replaces the view of the neighbourhood as a single entity concept with overtones on the promotion of neighbourliness and community feeling. Again, the key word is social evolution, not social engineering: the aim should be to provide a satisfactory physical form to the neighbourhood so that particular communities may develop their own characteristics of social organization.

In short, we may recall the words of the Reith Committee on New Towns (1946): 'Our responsibility . . . is to conduct an essay in civilization, by seizing an opportunity to design, solve and carry into execution for the benefit of coming generations, the means for a happy and gracious way of life.'[14] The ends may be similar, but the means are different because assumptions have changed about the functioning of communities and the nature of society.

Having determined an approach to neighbourhood planning in general we can now turn our attention to specific questions which may arise within the neighbourhood where social planning policies may play a particular part. A number of examples can illustrate how the social planner will now be involved in technical objectives far beyond layout exercises in physical design terms.

The question of social mix for example is important. This has been a live issue throughout the history of neighbourhood planning, and early evidence from New Towns suggested that social engineering was to entail the close intermixture of different social elements within society: 'If the community is to be truly balanced, so long as social classes exist all must be represented on it. A contribution is needed from every type and class of person; the community will be poorer if all are not there, able and willing to make it' were the words the Final Report of the New Towns Committee.[15] All this sounds rather dated now in the light of events during the last twenty years, but the spectre of large one-class estates producing a coarse grain in the internal structure of towns still haunts the imagination of those who fear and deplore the social segregation which might result. The evidence of American towns is clear whereby (admittedly under different circumstances) downtown areas and the suburbs are sharply differentiated by ethnic, religious and social class divisions.

Social mobility, interchange and communications between communities break down isolation, misunderstanding and prejudice in society and remove the grossest inequalities of opportunity. A very careful balance is required therefore between on the one hand allowing for the legitimate social and housing aspirations of different sections of the community, and on the other permitting residential areas of a particular homogeneous character and of such a size that they are separated from other areas of differing character. As Wilbur Thompson has written, 'Residential segregation by income class is transformed by sheer size from the relatively innocent act of pursuing personal living amenities into a major impediment to social interaction among classes and to the development of human resources.'[16] There can be no clear-cut rules of planning practice about this. Each situation will demand its own interpretation; a homogeneous community in one locality may be thought of undesirable size, but not so in another. This calls for the greatest sophistication by the planner in allocating land of certain size and shape for suitably sized residential areas, where differing social class compositions might emerge, within the context of a particular urban area.

Social planning policies for the neighbourhood extend to the micro-level in the design of the built environment. For instance, there is design for visibility and for privacy by allowing for maximum contact between individuals, but yet ensuring privacy when demanded. People may like both to see and to be seen by their immediate neighbours, and informal contacts are appreciated and desirable. On the other hand there are others who prefer to keep their social experience within the family or amongst chosen friends or organizations, and for these, privacy in and around the house is important.

Then there is design for facilitating casual contacts away from the home but within the immediate surroundings. This might be achieved by a layout of well-planned footpaths, open space and children's play spaces (Plate VI). Recent research has thrown more light on the catchment area of children's playgrounds: a threshold of about 400 yards seems to operate for most ages where provision in the form of both formal and informal equipment is available.[17] The provision of these areas regularly throughout a residential area at say half-mile intervals seems most important.

There are also design principles conducive to the formation of informal adult groups. Many adults, especially women, make initial contact with each other through children, a universal common interest. The simple provision of equipment such as seats or benches in areas such as toddlers' playgrounds is an important supplement to the more obvious provision of adult recreation rooms in clubs and community buildings.

An example of an attempt to integrate many of these social planning policies in design terms may be seen in the Park Hill development, Sheffield (Plate VII). The architect's concept was for a system of broad street decks to run through the blocks of buildings so making it possible to go from one end to another without going down to ground level. These decks are big enough to admit tradesmen's pedestrian-controlled delivery trucks but not vehicles of other types. The doors of all the apartments open on to one or other of these decks so that they become the backbone of both social communication and social grouping: 'at corners and other natural points of human aggregation, kids play, mums natter, teenagers smooch and squabble, dads hash over union affairs and the pools'.[18]

This was a social solution for high-density development. In areas of low-density housing the effective unit for neighbourliness is different, and likely to be a small section of a street, cul-de-sac or small square of perhaps only ten to twenty houses. Design for privacy in the external environment will be critical.

Social planning also extends to the provision of facilities and services within the neighbourhood. Early neighbourhood planning exercises were keen to regularize the approach with a standard provision of shops, community buildings, schools, service industry and open space. In practice there is a good deal of *ad hoc* provision which betrays not only the consequences of changing circumstances but also a good deal of uncertainty about what policies might now be adopted.

More research is clearly indicated and the recent work of Lee is instructive. For example there is always the vexed question of catchment areas: if a certain facility is provided will it be used adequately, and if so by whom? One investigation by Lee has been into the provision of facilities for further education.[19] In this case data were collected from a college providing a wide range of adult education near the centre of a provincial city of 85,000 population.

The results of the survey showed that enrolment rates were unaffected by convenience, and an implication was that adult education facilities might be provided at least five miles apart without loss of potential students. Taking this point further, if 'serious' activities do not respond to convenience, then the neighbourhood can hardly be an adequate catchment area. This suggests that the policy of combining both light and serious activities in a neighbourhood building may need re-examination.

This study stemmed from earlier work of Lee into the optimum provision and siting of social clubs in Cambridge.[20] An important finding was that social buildings might be scattered both among and within residential neighbourhoods and might be reasonably multiplied 'up to limits that will be set by the economy rather than by any fear of redundancy'. The basis of this conclusion was that the hypothesis that people might be divided into either 'joiners' or 'non-joiners' was untenable. In other words, the number of consumers should rise by the greater provision of social buildings—a highly relevant view, if, as we have asserted, the promotion of social participation is fundamental to the objectives of social planning.

The social planner will make a maximum contribution and draw together many of the aspects described above in a comprehensive way when he considers the social needs of new communities. There is still much left to be desired in the performance of local authorities in this connection, as is suggested in a recent report of a subcommittee of the Central Housing Advisory Committee.[21]

If we take as an example the instance of an overspill development, a brief review of some of the factors involved will indicate the social planning field. In the first place it is clearly necessary to establish which types of families are to be housed, especially their age, size and income group. The age factor is crucial, for failure to ensure as high a degree of 'balance' as possible will cause strains on the education and health services. An abnormal age structure, characterized by extreme youthfulness, will give rise to problems of 'peaks' and 'troughs'. There will be an immediate need for example to meet a peak demand for maternity, child welfare and welfare services. This will be followed by a peak demand for primary schools, then secondary schools, youth services, employment of school leavers and finally 'second-generation' housing. Providing for these peaks is one problem, but the peaks are followed by troughs where excess capacity is revealed.

But there are other reasons for age balance. There is for example social benefit in having middle-aged and elderly households in a new community because these householders have more time and experience to give to community affairs. Additionally, a mixture of household types enables a wider range of dwelling types to be provided, which is beneficial when the community matures.

Another aspect of overspill development is when the community is to be a dormitory one. Post-war development has shown the great difficulties which exist in securing industrial mobility of an appropriate scale to meet the needs of peripheral communities. There are immediate problems of the expenses of journey to work and the lack of employment opportunities for women and school leavers. This has implications for the income groups of the households to be accommodated and the rent levels to be demanded. If new, or re-housing is to result in a sharp fall in a family's economic surplus, it is pertinent to inquire where economies are to be made and which sections of the household might bear the brunt.

Planning for the social needs of a new community has to be a fully comprehensive exercise. A major characteristic of the development will be the relative lack of an established social fabric with its own customs, traditions and institutions, and there will be a demand for community buildings and facilities. Health and education will be critical services and closest liaison between Health and Education Authorities, the Executive Council, the Regional Hospital Board and various social work agencies will be required. All this of course is in addition to the many community facilities which are necessary for new arrivals, and for which a considerable co-ordination of services is required.[22]

Housing

It will be clear that social planning at the neighbourhood level will include policies regarding housing. It will be recalled that poor housing was an early object of attention by social reformers, and while extreme inadequacies have been removed there are still wide inequalities in housing provision. But the housing question contains a large number of complex issues concerned with matters such as housing administration, public health and deeply rooted political attitudes. Housing however is central to the built environment, and the social planner should offer a co-ordinating role over the whole field as well as providing a particular contribution in certain sectors. There is certainly a great need for drawing together a highly fragmented sphere of activity. There has been Government 'interference' in housing for a century, even before the Public Health Act, 1875, which was concerned, *inter alia,* with building construction and the layout of dwellings. The last fifty years have seen the inception of rent control and slum clearance, and since the war, local authorities have both extended old responsibilities and assumed new ones, for example in the form of concern for the housing of special groups, such as the elderly, and for the improvement of older housing. The time is very appropriate for co-ordination of housing policies as currently administered by different departments and committees of local authorities; in this, the role of the planner as well as the specialist social planner will be crucial.

One immediate field of interest concerns the process of re-development and the question of improvement to dwellings. The last fifteen years have been marked especially by very active slum clearance programmes and in this period substantial areas of our larger towns and cities, especially those with an industrial heritage of extensive nineteenth-century development, have largely been refashioned, socially and physically. The planner's role will clearly continue to be central to this exercise whereby new residential areas are designed, new elements of townscape built and new communities created and provided for.

The range of problems related to urban renewal will be examined in a later section, but one particular aspect of the housing question is relevant here. This concerns the improvement of dwellings as opposed to demolition and clearance. It is now generally recognized that in housing, far greater investment now needs to be devoted to improvement of dwellings as opposed to clearance and rebuilding. Perhaps too much emphasis has been put on 'new development', and we do well to recall that new dwellings add less than two per cent to the national housing stock each year. The majority of the population will never live in a new house, just as the majority of schoolchildren will never attend a new school or the majority of the ill will never go to a new hospital.

The composition of the total dwelling stock of a particular area from the point of view of size, type, tenure and price is an issue for the social planner because of its immediate relevance to housing satisfaction and availability of choice. Take for example the question of size of dwellings in terms of numbers of rooms: the proportion is frequently determined with only the minimum information concerning social or demographic needs. In the public sector the architect may interpret the requirements of the housing manager, who bases his estimate perhaps on intuitive reflection resting on experience or the results of a latest survey from a clearance area. In the private sector the architect designs to sell, quickly and easily, with the result that the most flexible unit, the three-bedroomed dwelling, is most popularly built. In short, this aspect of composition of dwelling stock is frequently a 'hit and miss' affair as a technical exercise, but we can show that it demands much greater planning analysis.

It should be a fundamental part of a local authority's housing objectives to secure a size distribution of the total stock of dwellings which is in balance with its household size distribution; if there is imbalance, there are unmet social needs. In attempting this exercise a statistical study of some complexity is demanded, and the planner has already made a contribution in this field, as suggested in a recent study in respect of Sunderland.[23]

A research methodology, worked out for the situation at Newcastle, broke new ground, and this might be briefly mentioned.[24] Newcastle has a marked imbalance in its dwelling size structure; in 1961, thirty-eight per cent of the City's dwellings contained three habitable rooms or less, and in consequence there was marked overcrowding where households of above-average size were living in such small dwellings. In recent years important trends have been noted, chiefly that due to slum clearance the proportion of small dwellings was decreasing and that there was an overall desire for more living space, reflected in a general 'drift' towards larger dwellings in spite of a decrease in average household size.

The research exercise concluded that the size-distribution of dwellings in the City is so distorted at present that the numbers of one- and two-roomed dwellings, even allowing for considerable clearance by 1981, exceed the demand for them at 1981. The study went further to provide a policy framework indicating the proportion of dwellings of different sizes which should be built in a given period. There were a number of implications for housing policies, quite apart from the building programme, but from the social planning point of view the essence of the exercise was that greater choice and opportunity was to be afforded in the housing market.

Beyond this, the planner's concern with housing will involve him with a number of complex and interrelated issues; few specific questions will be as relatively 'self-contained' as the one just reviewed. Because a person's dwelling constitutes an immediate physical environment, its importance for the social planner cannot be minimized: it is here that the key to environmental determinism was supposed by the early reformers. One can appreciate why the social engineer is by inclination so keen to control housing supply, its design and occupation. But this is scarcely possible even if it were desirable. So for the social planner, who sees his role primarily as a provider for social evolution, his work must be concerned more with seeing that in broad terms housing requirements are met.

The 'broad brush' strategy will also suggest to the planner the need to evaluate underlying national or at least regional trends in housing which may reflect the desires and aspirations of people at large. These may be extremely powerful forces and it is clearly inadvisable to ignore them. An important issue for example is the current growth in owner-occupation. This has been one of the most remarkable changes in housing since the end of the last war, for in 1947 only a quarter of householders in Great Britain owned their houses, a proportion increasing to two-fifths by 1961 and currently approaching a half.

The great attractions of owner-occupation are well known in providing security, freedom, pride of possession and in representing a considerable investment and a valued status symbol. The consequences have been immense because there is now a new and unexpected factor in the planning of residential areas. For example, overspill calculations are severely affected because that sector of the population which could at one time have confidently been expected to constitute 'planned overspill', i.e. destined to be housed in a local authority dwelling, may now be 'voluntary movement' securing housing tenure of another form. The desire for owner-occupation is seen at its most forceful with the demand for new houses; as these are more readily provided, and at lower cost, in urban peripheries rather than in inner areas of towns, this factor is clearly important in the vigour of contemporary urban spread.

Comprehensive housing policies cannot ignore the question of rent. A radical reassessment is demanded because at the present time the situation is that families are being helped differently and unfairly. Once again this is a field where the social planner will require a familiarity and understanding of situations not previously thought pertinent. The cost of housing is clearly one of these. The planner will not be called upon to bear responsibility for rent policies; this issue clearly lies in other quarters, but he will be expected to offer a co-ordinating role and ensure that rent policies do not conflict with other aspects of social policy.

A local authority with a large stock of pre-war houses can, because of inflation, make a considerable 'profit' from the rents of these houses, and by 'pooling' reduce the rents of newer houses. A very different situation obtains with New Towns, where rents accordingly are very much higher. In the private rented sector, there is a confused situation, with however most of the dwellings subject to either rent control or rent regulation. Owner-occupiers are helped financially by tax reliefs, and the new option-mortgage scheme extends this assistance to buyers where incomes are too low to benefit from normal reliefs. In addition to these various forms of assistance with housing costs there are households on Supplementary Benefits who are eligible for rent assistance. But still, those families who need most help do not necessarily get it, particularly the young family, the migrant family moving between local authorities, and the immigrant from overseas, especially if he is coloured.

Another relevant issue will be the role of housing associations, the so-called 'third arm' in housing which it is hoped may answer the requirements of those whose needs are patently not met at the present time. Research and patient experiment with the workings of housing associations to see how they best develop in a British situation is urgently needed; one recent study has been concerned with provision for the elderly.[25]

So in conclusion, the social planner's interest is with the broad, structural provision of housing—dwelling sizes, costs and trends in tenure for example—rather than in dwellings as a medium to influence behaviour. At the same time particular aspects in housing which may seem to be highly related to social problems will require special attention: the elimination of poor housing and overcrowding as well as multi-occupation in its extreme form where it is accompanied by inadequate management will be achieved through public health action. The social planner's contribution here will be to continue to draw attention to the social factors surrounding poverty of housing conditions and to relate them to the incidence of wider environmental criteria.

Urban Renewal

The inner areas of our towns and cities present the planner with a series of complex problems. As far as the improvement of the physical environment and the replacement of housing stock through clearance and new building are concerned, this is a familiar exercise and need not be especially stressed here. As a purely 'physical' operation it has proved to be well within the technical competence of the planner. Most local authorities have now had ample experience of 'programming' a number of different technical processes within a time scale; the rehousing of many thousands of slum families has been effected; and new communities have been established in environments of quite different form.

There cannot of course be any complacency in the results achieved. The socio-psychological effects of relocation have been imperfectly understood, and rehousing has often been a very blunt instrument in the search for improvement. As Hilda Jennings puts it, '. . . compulsory rehousing . . . entails a heavy responsibility on the society in whose name the compulsion is applied. Because of the complex nature of individuals it has to be recognized that they will require more than the physical basis for a satisfying life to compensate as far as possible for the non-material satisfactions which they may have lost.'[26]

But a quite different planning exercise is necessary for those inner urban areas where improvement and retention of existing dwellings are judged to be appropriate, rather than clearance and rebuilding. Here, because of the retention of existing communities there are dependent social issues, and a very different approach is required to marry the objectives of physical and social planning. The inner areas show distinct ecological characteristics and far too little is known about them for planning policies at present conceived to have much chance of success.

It would be invidious to single out any particular local autority's proposals for residential rehabilitation to demonstrate the lop-sided approach to the problem, but most of them are distressingly similar in omitting crucial areas of investigation. Often the most meticulous surveys are prepared of physical conditions, but social surveys are virtually ignored. A typical local authority report might begin by showing that a substantial proportion of its area's dwellings lacked one or more of the basic amenities of flush toilet, fixed bath and hot and cold water; and by indicating the slow rate of both slum clearance and revitalization through improvement grants, that a new injection into the pace of environmental improvement is necessary. The survey will then indicate the number of dwellings in the area selected, and their amenities; environmentally it will reveal such things as lack of open space, poor garaging facilities, a criss-cross of residential streets allowing an incoherent traffic pattern, and a rash of non-conforming uses such as timber yards, decorators' merchants, car dealers and service industries. The proposals will usually be on the lines of a rationalization of traffic flows, permitting the closing of certain streets, greater parking facilities, additional children's play areas, the clearing out of problem land activities, and landscaping improvements. The actual implementation of housing improvement is the weak point, and these problems are skirted round with hints of new legislation. Finally, as a public document artists' 'before-and-after' impressions suggest the new possibilities afforded: from depressing slum conditions, a pedestrian area emerges with no hint of the unmanageable or the undesirable. In all this the social environment is virtually ignored: as far as the end product is concerned, it is assumed that the new area will be peopled by those who derive the greatest satisfaction from their new conditions, but this apart, a deep understanding of the social conditions of the area selected for improvement is lacking.

This is an instance where a 'broad brush' interest will not suffice; here the social planner's role is concerned with detail at the micro-level. It is true that in recent years there has been a significant advance in housing policies for inner areas. A number of progressive local planning authorities have extended these beyond the initial stage of simply recognizing slum clearance areas and having virtually no proposals for the remainder of the housing stock. Many now recognize gradations in housing fitness and standards as for example the following:

1. Severe unfitness, clearance within a short period of years.
2. Significant evidence of unfitness, certain deficiences in household arrangements, dwellings of short life; these are dwellings for clearance but in the interim it is worth spending some money in patching and mending, together with important (but minimal in cost) environmental improvements. This is 'short-term revitalization (rehabilitation)'.
3. Old dwellings, not yet unfit. The chief shortcoming here is creeping decay caused by inadequate management, and inadequacy of dwelling stock in terms of internal facilities, and the poverty of the total environment. The usually held view is that it is economically and socially advantageous to prevent

the onset or furtherance of physical decay by the provision of new amenities and modernization of dwellings and environment. It is in this field that the principal debate has been about the merits of an improvement policy, and the machinery whereby it can be achieved, in order that these areas might have a guaranteed life of say up to thirty years or more. This is 'long-term revitalization (rehabilitation).'

These categories are based on standards of physical fitness. There are of course other categories, for example of function, social composition, and tenure, the whole of which might determine the practicability or timing of certain courses of action. These other criteria do not yet form the usual basis of intervention in twilight area housing; one of the shortcomings at the present time seems to be that the focussing of attention on standards of fitness results in other very important issues being insufficiently considered.

These other issues are quite critical, because the point has been made previously that it is impossible to make adequate physical plans for a community without at the same time recognizing the social characteristics of the community itself. In other words, we must be sure who we are planning for in the planning of twilight areas. The most careful surveys will be required to elicit this evidence: they may be the young, newly married and mobile, *en route* when financial circumstances permit for suburbia; they may be the elderly, residents of long standing, trapped in an area of change because they lack the economic means of escape and the psychological strength to move from an area of long-standing familiarity; they may be coloured immigrants finding a place to live near their own kin; they may be the poor, the handicapped and the underprivileged whose housing requirements are not met elsewhere; or they may be the transient who have no long-term interest in the area.

Relevant planning policies should be twofold: firstly to secure environmental improvement as an exercise in design terms to make beautiful cities and secondly to improve the lot of individuals and communities, aiming to secure happiness and satisfaction. It is in the planning of inner areas that these two policies are the most difficult to harmonize, because the best physical solution from the design point of view may be at variance with the immediate interest and capacities of the community in question. It is in these areas where the best may patently be the enemy of the good. This in fact may be the hardest, but most salutary contribution that the social planner can make to planning, namely that planning proposals for inner areas may conceivably stop far short of the most satisfactory from the point of view of urban design and environmental quality; uniformity of residential standards is not sacrosanct for the social planner, because for him the essential dictate in twilight areas must be the contemporary social requirements of individual groups within an existing community, not an idealized future situation. In this particular exercise planning is urged to become gradualist and seek to achieve advanced environmental quality progressively, and not as a result of a once and for all attack.

It will be appreciated that this attitude will be regarded by many as a let-down or a sell-out to the already underprivileged communities in twilight areas—why should they be denied environmental living conditions which are adopted without question in the planning of new communities? There is no answer to this except as seen in fullness of time, and in balancing the practical advantages and disadvantages of a situation at the present day. John Betjeman in *The Town Clerk's Views* caricatured the planner's desire for things new:

> Hamlets which fail to pass the planners' test
> Will be demolished. We'll rebuild the rest
> To look like Welwyn mixed with Middle West.[27]

Social planning does not necessarily aim at once for the ultimate solution: it need not necessarily be concerned with the new and the best for in certain circumstances the most satisfactory answer is probably simply to make things better—to relieve the grossest inequality in living conditions and to open up new areas of opportunity.

The great need in inner areas at the present time is to know more about their social composition, their role in the total urban context, and the socio-economic characteristics of the communities. There is a range of research questions which needs clarification for every twilight area planning project, because the main feature of inner areas is not their homogeneity but the internal differences within them.

An examination of the process of change will be important both within twilight areas and between them and other sectors of the city. What changes have taken place, and how and why? Why have some areas changed more rapidly than others? What are the critical issues in precipitating change? Why do some areas 'go downhill' at a certain time?

Similarly, there must be an examination of the social problems within the area. This will identify the facts of location of social problems which may exist. To what extent are there concentrations of the elderly, the poor, the immigrant, or the problem family? Does this suggest that twilight areas have a social role as 'residual areas'?

There must also be a detailed evaluation of relevant characteristics. What sort of broad homogeneity exists? How significant are the internal differences? How socially distinctive is the area under consideration? How self-contained is it from the point of view of employment, recreation, shopping and social facilities, social contacts and so on? What exposure is there to other environments and how far is there isolation from other parts of the city? What satisfactions are expressed with twilight areas as areas in which to live? What are the aspirations of the people? What are their attitudes to housing, environment, social change and to moving to other districts? What new resources and facilities are needed? How important is the supply of cheap old houses, and the supply of privately rented houses?

These are some of the social questions to be answered as part of a twilight area project. There are thorough investigations to be made too into the physical and economic environments, so much so that it will be readily apparent that such an urban renewal exercise must of necessity be a major and comprehensive undertaking. Altogether a different approach to twilight area planning is required than has been achieved so far: many more skills and resources need to be brought to bear, and social considerations given far greater prominence.

Approaches adopted so far in this country have been understandably faltering. The Rye Hill project in Newcastle has been widely publicized as one of the first attempts at a comprehensive rehabilitation project for an inner area of a major city[28] (Plates VIII and IX). As a physical design solution within the context of Newcastle's pioneering efforts towards a comprehensive housing policy it was a trend-setter now followed in many parts of the country. But as a social planning exercise it might now, with hindsight, be considered crude and clumsy; this is because in the first place insufficient was known about the community concerned and secondly there was insufficient flexibility in the housing and environmental solutions bearing in mind the needs and restricted expectations of the residents.

But lessons are learned from such experiments: '. . . an approach is needed which builds on the social structure of the community, and seeks not to dominate but rather to capture the rhythm and style of life, replacing service provision with a plan and program that would maximize opportunities and create an environment in which cultural values and human aspirations can be realized'.[29] It is necessary to identify the dynamic factors that operate in twilight areas. These areas are not accidental phenomena but are the creation of broad social, physical and economic processes. Rye Hill in Newcastle is an underprivileged area with a host of deep, related problems. Planning intervention within the context of housing improvement has of necessity to be of the most sophisticated kind. Most large cities with twilight areas have these problems, and so far we have done little more than fumble with techniques of environmental management.

Increasingly, inner areas are housing the disadvantaged elements of the population, those who lack resources needed to compete successfully with other groups in the community and those who lack influence over the institutional channels whereby such resources are distributed. Social planning policies therefore need to be orientated to reflect the needs and aspirations of the various groups within the population. They also need to show an understanding of the web of institutional arrangements, life patterns and channels of, and obstructions to, opportunity and choice within twilight areas. Only in this way will it be possible to relay a social foundation for co-ordinating public and private institutional patterns, freeing new channels of resources. At the same time, physical planning goals will seek to procure environmental changes which will curtail past constraints and open up new improvements. In this there will have to be a willingness to overlook idealized planning standards more applicable in other communities. The result would be 'an indivisible social and physical planning process focussing on these factors and forces which limit resources and choice rather than on the application of social and physical planning assumptions based on ostensibly desirable styles of family life, individual behaviour, and spatial arrangements'.[30]

In the remoulding of the physical, social and institutional life of the chronic problem area, selective aid should be channelled, and perhaps there is need for a new concept of 'disaster area' status for the grossly underprivileged and social problem area.

These areas should have the highest priority for the allocation of social welfare and educational services. A start has at least been made in the Plowden Report,[31] which argues that the gap between the educational opportunities of the most and least fortunate children should be closed. *Inter alia*, the Report recommended that as a matter of national policy 'positive discrimination' should favour schools in neighbourhoods where children are most severely handicapped by home conditions. A start should be made as soon as possible by giving priority to the most severely deprived pupils, starting with two per cent of the pupils and building up to ten per cent over five years. What has been suggested for education needs to be achieved on the broadest social front.

Individual Problem Groups

As we have seen, many of the objectives of social planning are met by measures which operate broadly across society, whereby opportunity, choice and freedom in the widest sense will be provided. But there will still be certain areas of disadvantage which will be untouched by the redistribution and enhancement of opportunity. These will require special recognition by the social planner, and while many of the individual policies in respect of them will be carried out in the general field of social administration and not by planners at all in the professional sense, such is the interrelated nature of the problem that he must continue to be involved by virtue of his co-ordinating function.

We have already seen for example that problem families have been the object of study in Newcastle by a broadly disciplined working party where the planner had much to contribute.[32] For example he identified the distribution of problem families in the City and related certain areas of concentration to other factors under the broad heading of social malaise. One of the measures of a range of policies drawn up to meet the situation was for a Family Service Unit to be set up in the City, and clearly at this stage of implementation the practical work of the professional planner as well as the specialist social planner terminates. But in any comprehensive social service the marrying of physical and social policies is a never-ending process and there will be a need for a continual interdisciplinary working arrangement.

With this wide brief the planner's contribution is considerably extended. Juvenile delinquency for example becomes a matter not only for the probation officer or the social case worker, but the planner too, because a clinical approach to delinquency which sees it in relation to factors resulting in a particular person breaking the law is supplemented by a community approach by virtue of environmental factors and social setting. In other words, we have to think not only of remedial measures for the individual, but also in terms of remedying the defects in the economic and social base of society.

This new involvement for planning, because of a concern with society as well as the physical environment, will lead to comprehensive policy making for a number of community groups, such as the elderly, the homeless, the vagrants and so on. Another which has been the subject of study at Newcastle is prostitution. A Working Party was set up by the Town Planning Committee to study this problem because of the difficulties which were thought likely to arise in implementing the planning proposals for the Rye Hill area, where a substantial number of prostitutes were known to be located. The problem was one of seeking environmental improvements contemporaneously with a new-found social standing for the area. It is of course possible as a social engineering exercise to remove prostitution from any area by virtue of a policy of scatter, once the local authority has a major share in ownership of dwellings (and therefore control over tenancies). But this is not possible without a similar situation being created in another district. This is a highly pertinent problem in twilight areas, some of which by their very nature tend to assimilate deviants and social problems of this nature, and where, as areas of transition, patterns of social blight tend to be migratory. This is a good example of how interrelated are the problems of the inner areas of cities and what careful and comprehensive studies of the process of urban decay are required.

But of all these examples perhaps one group of social disadvantage stands out, namely the coloured immigrant. As with many such groups, they are primarily located in inner areas, and the suggestion has already been made that the comprehensive planning of these areas will necessitate studies of the social, physical and economic environment; in this, the understanding of immigrant groups and their aspirations will be crucial.

To a large extent the problems of accommodating the immigrant stem from the clash of traditional cultures. There are cultural differences between the host community and the immigrant as well as between the various immigrant groups; there are differences in attitudes towards marriage and the role of women in society, towards children and family life and towards work and social status. Hence there is concern with the meaning of 'integration', and the kind of society towards which our aim should be directed. This allows the planner to be something rather more than a co-ordinator; by virtue of his idealism he has something to champion—in this case a view of urban society, rich in diversity, and where barriers to opportunity are removed. The hope must be that the immigrant groups will retain some of their cultural traits, but that at the same time the members of these groups will join other groups of the host community, whether it be the trade unions, sports clubs, political parties or churches. Integration in this sense is assimilation. As Philip Mason has written: 'The richer we are in groups and subgroups the better; let there be societies for the encouragement of Basque cookery and Welsh madrigals, Indian workers' associations, West Indian cricket clubs and pentecostal churches. Let there be calypsos and steel bands; let Pakistanis meet for a mash'ara (their equivalent to an Eisteddfod). But let no one be denied entry to one group on the sole ground that he belongs to another.' [33]

With this objective (which builds on the western tradition of consensus rather than conflict in society) it is clear that an underlying goal should be to facilitate the mutual understanding and respect for the traditions of both the immigrants and the host community. This will be achieved by fostering communications between social groups and by providing facilities for the expression of minority views. Such policies might include an increased provision of English classes for immigrants, the encouraged use of public libraries, the appointment of liaison officers to work with the Chief Constable to do 'all-round jobs' in schools and courts, the appointment of an immigrant liaison officer to promote community development, integration and casual contact between immigrant groups and the host community, and special help for immigrants in finding sites for their special social and religious buildings. Additional policies have to be made to counter the fact of underprivilege. This will mean particularly an end to discrimination in housing, education and employment.

The immigrant groups are largely located in the environmentally disadvantaged areas of cities. One such area, Sparkbrook, has been described by Rex and Moore;[34] within it, Claremont Road was pictured in detail (Plate X):

About half the houses have drab, peeling paintwork, and the

others are painted in various bright blues, purples and reds. Two houses have every brick painted red and the pointing and stonework white. The front doors stand open on long, dark passageways. The narrow pavements are uneven and cracked where the roots of the trees have pushed them up, and the narrow road is blocked at a number of points by cars in various states of repair. . . . Gardens have overgrown hedges, a few dead shrubs and hardened patches of grass and hard earth. There is broken glass and torn paper on the pavement and in the road. A few milk and beer bottles are lying in the gutter.

From one window comes the sound of steel band music, from another the latest Urdu pop song. Laughter and animated conversation issue from a dozen windows, the sounds of a family row from another. People are eating behind one window, washing behind another, and just looking out of a third.

These are the facets of urban change and rapid environmental decay which surround the living conditions of an immigrant group in a particular part of Birmingham, but they are typical for many communities. Housing policies for immigrants are inescapably connected with overall strategies for twilight areas; the most complex problems of cities are here, and the facts of social disadvantage are exacerbated in conditions of poor housing.

Social Administration

Important agents in social planning are the public authorities, voluntary associations and relevant bodies like the churches; these act through the institutional framework and they channel technical and human resources to people and groups in society.

In this area of operation the social planner's role will be to act primarily as a co-ordinator and as a source of intelligence for a number of people and organizations from a wide background. This will not be an easy field, but if confidences can be gained, then a marked contribution should be made. Perhaps at the outset the social planner should indicate that he does not see himself in any way operating as a social worker or as a community organizer, but entirely in a supportive or integrative way, providing co-ordinated information and facilitating work between a number of different social organizations.

The prize in this new field will be to secure a greater joint effectiveness of the institutional framework. We have already seen that this is most necessary in new communities where established channels are absent, and in twilight areas where the channels are frequently precluded from reaching those most in need. There are gaps here in provision which the social planner will be anxious to close: one is in the field of social work, another concerns the provision of community facilities, and another, organizational management.

With regard to social work, this is a process involving a range of workers with distinctive skills. For example, case work is a personal service provided for individuals who require skilled assistance in resolving material or personality problems within a family or community setting. In group work, on the other hand, case workers have a relationship not solely with individuals but also with members of a group. Even wider needs are served by community organizations, less personal than the other services. Another aspect of social work in the broad sense might be seen in a different structure. At one level there is the adult education movement and the youth service; then there are voluntary groups and societies such as the work of residential settlements and the community association movements; and, also there is the work of the churches. Local authorities are playing an increasingly active part in community organization, recognizing that the total needs of society and the serving of those needs call for co-ordination of activity on a scale not yet achieved. It is here that the social planner may develop an embryo role, now being shared by a number of local authority departments.

But changing circumstances also demand new experiments, and research is called for. An action research project in Bristol for example, conducted on the basis not only of securing and processing information but on positively influencing social conditions at the same time, has indicated that improved social relationships can be achieved even in very difficult social circumstances by trained social workers if they are able to concentrate on a particular field of endeavour.[35] One of the recommendations from this work was that, as a matter of considerable urgency, there should be serious and sustained experiments in appropriate methods of gaining contact with 'hard-to-reach' youth. Ideally, it was felt, there should have been a trained social worker for each of the gangs in the neighbourhood. They also suggested that there should be a community organizer with a roving commission to learn about the area and its people, to identify their needs, to gain a personal knowledge of the leaders (formal and informal) in

F

the area, and then, by group work to work with people where hostile feelings are evident, with a view to ameliorating difficult social conditions in the area. Such research into aspects of social work is so far the exception rather than the rule, but clearly there is the need for further research programmes, the findings to be processed by the social planner in his additional role of 'intelligence co-ordinator'.

The need for a social worker to help to develop personal relationships has been recognized in New Town development. J. H. Nicholson, in a report to the National Council of Social Services, reported that experience had shown that a Social Development Officer or a Neighbourhood Worker is needed in all new developments and that such an officer might well work with a committee of statutory and voluntary bodies concerned with community service in the area.[36] This observation is of relevance for virtually any major residential development either on the periphery of towns or in redevelopment areas.

This was borne out by the Central Housing Advisory Sub-Committee's report *The Needs of New Communities* which said that too often social aspects are considered only when problems arise, when the social worker or social scientist is then brought in to advise on how the social deficiencies can be made good.[37] The Sub-Committee maintained that just as landscape architecture needs to be considered at the planning stage of a scheme rather than after the development has taken place, so social planning must be an integral part of the whole planning and development process. That is a principle the social planner is happy to affirm.

There is a need too for these types of workers in established communities, especially in the twilight areas, marked perhaps by a concentration of social problems. Most cities will show a need for a community organizer in the worst areas of social and physical disadvantage, or for a group worker for particular families. A neighbourhood worker will be especially useful in areas selected for a particular planning exercise, for example for housing and environmental improvement whether through the Comprehensive Development Area procedure or that of a district plan or local plan.

Turning to the field of community facilities and services, the requirement for satisfactory provision has been highlighted in the needs of new housing areas. *The Needs of New Communities* pointed to a number of gaps in social provision in new and expanding communities and offered certain suggestions which might reasonably be taken up in social planning practice. For example, families moving to new areas may need assistance in 'settling in'. Careful preparations and good public relations are essential from the commencement of the building of any residential estate. An Arrivals Officer to welcome new tenants and deal with queries or complaints might be considered for large estates where a steady stream of incoming residents might be expected over a long period. Where a new estate is to be grafted on to an existing community, special attention will need to be given to factors promoting social integration.

Additional manpower resources will be found in the many voluntary organizations and the churches, all of which have a very important role to play in the development of new communities. Frequently the problem is not a case of finding adequate manpower to act in neighbourly or support-giving organizations, but of co-ordinating their activities in the most advantageous way and suggesting the best practical outlets for available energies. This freeing and easing of the channels of social communication might be the role of the Social Development Officer, referred to earlier.

From the point of view of community facilities, there will of course be a particular need of day nurseries, nursery school and pre-school play groups. At the present time there are difficulties in providing state nursery schools because of financial restrictions, but there are a number of possibilities for voluntary organizations. Provision for play spaces should of course form an integral part of the design of a neighbourhood. With regard to community buildings, we have already referred to recent research on which new ideas of standard of provision might be based (p. 135), but one early essential provision is a conveniently located central office from which varying kinds of personal help and advice can be sought. It is of course not only a case of providing buildings; the provision of sites can be equally important which will allow for the emergence of self-sponsored social clubs or special interest societies.

This particular aspect of community development will be readily familiar to the planner: concern for buildings is relevant to his 'allocating' role. But we might still remind ourselves of the words of the Sub-Committee: '. . . to build houses without parallel provision of community facilities and amenities will result in the unnecessary provision of social problems. This short-term saving in local authority expenditure may well turn out to be a false economy. What is saved and more may have to be spent by the personal social services in the rescue of families in distress.'[38]

With regard to possible gaps in the organizational management of social work we might refer to evidence from recent investigations in both Scotland and England and Wales and the reports of two important Committees.[39, 40] The present situation with regard to local authorities presents many defects. The organization of most local authority social work and welfare services was developed in a piecemeal manner and in response to the identification at different times of certain groups of people who have needed help. Welfare work has therefore developed in response to problems which have arisen or have been identified, and this inherited fragmentation now determines the characteristic approach and organization.

But this is in contrast to the interrelationships which exist in social problems. Social ills are closely connected with medical ills; personal problems are met with the support of other people; social problems are associated with others, and a number of different social services may be involved in remedial activity. But where there are separate services there may be confusion when help is required. As for the social workers, they all use basically the same skills, and when they are employed in separate services their efforts may not be deployed in the most effective and economical way. The social planner looks with interest at the Seebohm recommendations regarding the setting up of a new social service department.

He will also be concerned with the emphasis on the part which research must play in the creation and maintenance of an effective family service. 'Social planning is an illusion without adequate facts; and the adequacy of services mere speculation without evaluation.'[41] There will be a need for the collection of basic data as well as evaluation and analysis, and the Seebohm Report, favouring a research and intelligence unit to serve all departments of a local authority, goes on to comment that, 'It would be responsible for collecting information about the operation of the local public services, the community they serve and the needs with which they ought to be concerned. The social service department equally with the education, health, housing and planning department will have vital contributions to make to such a unit. . . .' This is extremely pertinent to one of the contributions in the role which we have outlined for the social planner.

Leisure and Recreation

Planning has always been very much concerned with the provision of facilities for recreation. The evolution of the planning movement was closely associated with the nineteenth-century fight for open spaces and commons in the reaction against unplanned urban development and its threat to the existence of natural amenities. 'Openness' was the early prize, and the Public Health Act, 1875, gave powers to local authorities to make provision for public walks and pleasure grounds. The pattern of need at that time was fairly parochial, but in the twentieth century the demand was for wider outdoor recreation and physical fitness. Playing grounds, gymnasia and camping grounds were the new needs, and provision for them was to be made ultimately through the Physical Training and Recreation Act, 1937. In the post-war period the National Parks and Access to the Countryside Act, 1949, and the Countryside Act, 1968, were designed to meet still-changing requirements. In this evolution the planner's role has been strengthened by virtue of wide powers over the control of land use: the planner's allocating function has ensured the provision of facilities, both urban and rural, at least in principle. In addition to this, 'standards' of provision have been drawn up in many cases, and these have become fossilized in the preparation of static planning schemes.

In planning for recreation there can no longer be any such heavy reliance on land use or standards of provision. The main reason for this is that the social and economic aspects of the underlying situation are radically different. Because of greater affluence, the effect of shorter working hours, enhanced personal mobility and exposure through education to a wider range of experience, the use of leisure time constitutes almost a new dimension in planning. Therefore in the preparation of a recreational planning policy framework it is fundamental to begin by recognizing the changing elements in demand.

Social factors have a considerable bearing on these, and here the specialist social planner can make a particular contribution to recreational planning. In the first place he will be able to show the special relevance of recreation and the use of leisure time in terms of opportunity and choice in society. Secondly, he will be able to apply the techniques of social analysis to any necessary reassessment of urban and rural provision. Thirdly he will be able to apply the same techniques to a monitoring of the use of facilities as an aid towards a process of continual revision of standards of provision. Lastly he will be able to show how a long-standing concern for recreation might now be widened into planning for leisure as a whole. Let us look in greater detail at this contributory role.

The contemporary challenge is to plan for, and at the same time educate society in the use of leisure time so that there is both the widest personal choice available and that the choice can be made with knowledge and purpose. It has not been until recently that the use of leisure time has been seen to have a function in society. There are a number of reasons for this. In the first place leisure time has been restricted for the bulk of the population, and opportunities have been lacking to explore new experiences and situations. Secondly, there has been an all-pervading puritan ethic which despised idleness and eulogized hard work.

But we might now consider the use of leisure time as a new area of personal freedom, assisting for example in the development of personal satisfactions. In this sense failure to plan adequately for leisure means the imposition of constraints on achieving personal satisfaction. Moreover, the use of leisure time should be meaningful in securing wider social contacts; one of the important aspects of contemporary recreation lies in its liberal and democratic value in eroding class and ethnic barriers.

The reasons for this new value attached to leisure time stem from changing circumstances, and are a product of the process of urbanization and industrialization. Contemporary urban man may have little opportunity to experience creative self-expression in his daily work and opportunity should be provided for the development of a leisure outlet which is both personal and purposive. The problems posed by work in a highly industrialized society are unlikely to be solved merely by escapist activities in leisure. Sport and physical recreation however provide a creative outlet, a medium of self-expression and a medium which will give social contacts, and for workers whose leisure-time interests are an extension of physical work there are a host of related and satisfying activities, for example in the form of woodworking or car repairing.

This recognition of leisure in a broad social context facilitates the preparation of guidelines for recreation planning policy. Basic questions will surround the provision of facilities, their nature and distribution, and in any evaluation of need, relevant social data will be important. As an example we might instance the standard of provision for playing fields, and the degree to which a reassessment might be thought overdue.

In 1925 the National Playing Fields Association formulated a standard for playing space of six acres per 1,000 population. The Association renewed this standard in 1955 and accepted its validity for the present day. The assumption was that facilities should be provided for organized games and outdoor physical recreation for 200 persons in every 1,000, and for this number six acres of playing fields were considered to be a minimum allocation, accommodating one senior football pitch, one junior football pitch or hockey pitch, a cricket table, one three-rink bowling green, and two tennis courts, together with a half-acre children's playground and a pavilion.

But Winterbottom in respect of Colchester has concluded that 'less than two acres per thousand population are needed in winter, as against the not ungenerous provision of two and a half acres for summer use, although most of this space was not being used for organized games during the latter season'.[42] Another challenge to the N.P.F.A. standard has come from Newcastle where a survey in 1966 found that only ten per cent of the population above 17 years of age would normally be engaged in outdoor games on a weekday summer evening, and that more than half of these were aged 50 and over, with golf and bowls the sports most in demand rather than other sports activities.[43] This is in contrast to the N.P.F.A. assumption that 20 per cent of the population aged between 10 and 40 would require provision for outdoor facilities, and on that basis alone it might be argued that Newcastle's provision should be reduced *pro rata* from six to three acres of playing fields per 1,000 population. There are other factors to take into account of course, for example strict comparability and the degree to which schoolchildren's needs are met by education playing fields, but this is an indication of the research which is needed, and the changes in policy which might stem from it.

This rethinking of the standards of provision for recreation implies an evaluation of future demand. Forecasting is a hazardous exercise, but because it is one where social trends are so important the social planner may make a useful contribution. In the balancing of supply and demand in the future for any group of activities in a particular geographical area, the crucial unknown is 'latent demand'. But because it is unrealistic to ask people what recreational activities they will be following in the future, or what they would like to follow, the question of statistical prediction of demand becomes important. This is based on the assumption that participation in a given activity is predictable from certain characteristics of the participant, and the nature and location of the home and area in which he lives.

Participation in recreation patterns seems to be structured through norms of behaviour which originate in a number of factors such as age, sex, marital status, social class, income, availability of time, motorization, educational attainment, susceptibility to status achievement, physical activity and personal vitality, family ties, religion and ethnic group. Participation is also of course affected by non-personal factors such as the physical characteristics of the dwelling and environment of the person concerned and its location relative to other urban areas and recreation areas concerned.

This suggests that individuals and households have characteristic recreation participation patterns which by and large within certain types of activity are predictable. In other words, present-day activities, seen in respect of personal profiles and the nature of the residential environment, might be projected by a process of simulation; future patterns of recreation activity might be evaluated by changing a number of variables such as social class, increased leisure time, motorization, and additional disposable income. In this way it will be possible to prepare sub-regional or regional models of recreational activity for a given date in the future. By a constant monitoring of the social trends affecting the variables a sophisticated evaluation of future requirements might be made. This will release the planner from undue reliance on *ad hoc* standards of provision and allow policies to be prepared, adaptive to changes in need.

As new sports facilities are provided it will constantly be necessary to monitor their use and impact on the community, in order to assist in the future planning of similar facilities. Here, a planner skilled in collecting and interpreting social data will again make a useful contribution. The provision of a sports hall may be cited as an example, and the opening of the Lightfoot Sports Centre in Newcastle in 1965 provided a good opportunity for survey. Personal and recreational profiles compiled from data provided by the users showed *inter alia* that a large proportion of the participants for such sports as badminton, basketball, table tennis and keep fit lived within half a mile of the Centre, but that for other sports such as gymnastics and golf the majority of the participants came from distances above one mile.

This suggested that the Centre acted in two quite different capacities. On the one hand it operated as a purely neighbourhood focus, but for specialisms it attracted people from much further afield. This contributes to the formulation of wider policy on the basis of a hierarchy of sports hall provision in an urban area to range from the district centre to the purely neighbourhood centre. If this is so, it confirms the need of provision on a lavish scale; if the full demand is ever likely to be met, the fullest use will have to be made of existing non-purpose-built buildings such as church halls, army drill halls and the like.

There will of course be the need to review constantly not only new but inherited facilities for sport and recreation. The traditional urban park is a case in point. A common hunch is that many city parks may be under-utilized by virtue of their location, restricted facilities, the activities of vandals and perhaps an apathy by parks superintendents towards experiment which might make them more attractive to a larger number of both children and adults. This suggests the need for research into the use made of urban parks, by whom, of what age, for what purpose, at what times of the day or week, and if they are not being visited, then what are the reasons?

The opportunities for survey into the use of recreation facilities are of course extensive. 'Turnstile surveys' are fairly easy to undertake and the possibilities of their contribution to policy making are immense. As an example we might refer to swimming baths. In an evaluation of demand much depends for this particular facility on the question of catchment area. It is a reflection of the retarded state of recreation research that so little reliable data is available from a variety of sources, of distances travelled to baths of different sizes and ancillary facilities, in different types of urban and rural areas; moreover, by whom, how frequently and at what times of the week or month. Current indications are that in urban areas at least a primary threshold level in provision occurs in a population range of 40,000–60,000. This is a wide threshold and the need for further information, including social data, is apparent.

The remaining contribution of the social planner in recreation planning policy will be to integrate the different aspects of recreation, indoor and outdoor, passive and active, into a general concept of leisure. This means that this branch of planning will be concerned with a very wide range of matters including the provision of playing fields, public open space, parks and allotments, buildings such as sports centres, swimming baths and those for commercial entertainment, and facilities such as golf courses and water-sports centres; also facilities for the arts, from theatres, cinemas, meeting halls, museums and libraries to art galleries. Until recently such a comprehensive concern has been precluded largely by reason of an absence of an integrative philosophy which accorded to recreation and leisure a positive function in society. But it has been prejudiced too from a local authority point of view by a division of administrative and executive responsibilities. In order to avoid duplication of effort and missed opportunities it is now necessary to ensure that the number of local authority departments and committees which are responsible for all the various aspects of provision is considerably reduced.

In the wider field of leisure (as opposed to physical recreation) the planner skilled at the collection of social data once again virtually has an open research field. We might give as an example the question of planning for theatres, so pertinent at a time when increasing local authority interest is being shown in their distribution and provision. There is obvious scope for research work into catchment areas, for when new theatres are being promoted or others taken over to save them from extinction, it is necessary to ascertain likely support in the future. Several audience surveys have been carried out recently in provincial and London suburban professional theatres, and although the evidence is somewhat conflicting, the usual theatre-going audience is younger than the total population, more middle class and consists of more women than men. But a national proportion for regular theatre-goers seems unreliable for use at a local level and there is scope for additive research into theatre catchment areas in terms of personal characteristics of the theatre-goer and area of residence.

REFERENCES TO CHAPTER 4

1. Donald L. Foley, 'British Town Planning: One Ideology or Three?' *British Journal of Sociology*, Vol. II, 1960.
2. Donald L. Foley, *op. cit.*
3. Constantinos A. Doxiadis, *Between Dystopia and Utopia*, The Trinity College Press, Hartford, 1966.
4. Margaret Mead, 'Megalopolis: is it Inevitable?', *Transactions of the Bartlett Society*, Vol. 3, 1964–5.
5. Walt Whitman, 'Song of Myself' in *Leaves of Grass*, New English Library, 1958.

6. Christopher Alexander, 'The City as a Mechanism for Sustaining Human Contact', in *Environment for Man. The Next Fifty Years*, editor William R. Ewald, Indiana University Press, 1967.

7. Philip Mason, 'What do we Mean by Integration?', *New Society*, 14 June 1966.

8. *Mobility and the North*, Technical Committee of Planning Officers, North Regional Planning Committee, July 1967.

9. Gordon E. Cherry, 'The Ambience of the North: the image of an unfavoured region', *Northern Architect*, July 1967.

10. *The West Midlands: a regional study*, Department of Economic Affairs, H.M.S.O., 1965.

11. *The West Midlands: patterns of growth*, West Midlands Economic Planning Council, H.M.S.O., 1967.

12. J. H. Forshaw and Patrick Abercrombie, *County of London Plan*, Macmillan, 1943.

13. R. Nicholas, *City of Manchester Plan*, Jarrold & Sons, 1945.

14. *Final Report of the New Towns Committee*, Cmd. 6876, H.M.S.O., 1946.

15. *Final Report of the New Towns Committee, op. cit.*

16. Wilbur R. Thompson, 'The Study of Urbanisation' in *Urban Economic Growth and Development in a National System of Cities*, editors P. M. Hauser and L. F. Schnore, John Wiley, 1965.

17. *The Playground Study: preliminary analysis*, Council for Children's Welfare, 1966.

18. Reyner Banham, *Guide to Modern Architecture*, The Architectural Press, 1962.

19. Terence Lee, 'A Null Relationship Between Ecology and Adult Education', *The British Journal of Educational Psychology*, Vol. XXXVI, February 1966.

20. Terence Lee, 'The Optimum Provision and Siting of Social Clubs', *Durham Research Review*, No. 14, September 1963.

21. *The Needs of New Communities*, a report on social provision in new and expanding communities prepared by a sub-committee of the Central Housing Advisory Committee, Ministry of Housing and Local Government, H.M.S.O., 1967.

22. *The First Hundred Families: community facilities for first arrivals in expanding towns*, Ministry of Housing and Local Government, H.M.S.O., 1965.

23. J. E. Barlow and G. I. Ramsdale, 'Balanced Population—an experiment at Silksworth, overspill township for Sunderland', *Journal of the Town Planning Institute*, Vol. 52, No. 7, July/August 1966.

24. Gordon E. Cherry, 'Assessment of Dwelling Size Requirements—Research Study of Need in Newcastle upon Tyne', *Chartered Surveyor*, Vol. 99, No. 12, June 1967.

25. Unity Stack, *The Development of a Housing Association*, Occasional Paper No. 1, Centre for Urban and Regional Studies, University of Birmingham, 1968.

26. Hilda Jennings, *Societies in the Making: a Study of Development and Redevelopment Within a County Borough*, Routledge, 1962.

27. John Betjeman, 'The Town Clerk's Views', in *John Betjeman's Collected Poems*, John Murray, 1958.
28. Wilfred Burns, *Report of Survey, Rye Hill Comprehensive Development Area, Written Analysis*, City and County of Newcastle upon Tyne, 1965.
29. Jack Meltzer and Joyce Whitley, 'Social and Physical Planning for the Urban Slum', in *Social Welfare and Urban Problems*, editor Thomas D. Sherrard, 1968.
30. Jack Meltzer and Joyce Whitley, *op. cit.*
31. *Children and their Primary Schools*, Report of the Central Advisory Council for Education (England), H.M.S.O., 1967.
32. *Report of Working Party on Problem Families*, Joint Sub-Committee as to Rehabilitation, City and County of Newcastle upon Tyne, January 1966.
33. Philip Mason, *op. cit.*
34. John Rex and Robert Moore, *Race, Community and Conflict*, Oxford University Press, 1967.
35. J. Spencer, *Stress and Release in an Urban Estate: a Study in Action Research*, Tavistock Publications, 1964.
36. J. H. Nicholson, *New Communities in Britain—Achievements and Problems*, National Council of Social Services, 1961.
37. *The Needs of New Communities, op. cit.*
38. *The Needs of New Communities, op. cit.*
39. *Social Work and the Community. Proposals for reorganizing local authority services in Scotland*, Scottish Education Department and the Scottish Home and Health Departments, Cmd. 3065, H.M.S.O., 1966.
40. *Report of the Committee on Local Authority and Allied Personal Social Services*, Cmd. 3703, H.M.S.O., 1968.
41. *Report of the Committee on Local Authority and Allied Personal Social Services, op. cit.*
42. D. M. Winterbottom, 'How Much Urban Open Space Do We Need?' *Journal of the Town Planning Institute*, Vol. 53, No. 4, April 1967.
43. Wilfred Burns, *Surveys into Leisure Activities*, City and County of Newcastle upon Tyne, September 1966.

5

Summary, Conclusions
and Implications

Consideration of the social aspects of town planning has led us to
examine the origins and the philosophical content of planning
itself and to review the scope of social planning as a particular
area of concern within the total discipline. The conclusions of
this long-overdue exercise are at once striking and the implications
far-reaching.

A principal starting point is that town planning rests funda-
mentally on a social base. Planning is not only a physical exercise
related to, for example, town building or allocations of land use;
it is also concerned with meeting social needs, aspirations and
interests, in part through intervention in the environment, and
this relationship affects the nature of the whole process.

As Benevolo has pointed out, modern town planning originated
in the last century when circumstances had crystallized sufficiently
not only to cause the discomfort, but also to provoke the protest
of the people involved. In this way the planning movement is 'an
integral part of the general attempt to extend the potential benefits
of the Industrial Revolution to members of all classes',[1] and has
therefore been a vital factor in the development of a democratic
society. Viewed in this way, the aim of planning is not 'the instant
achievement of formal perfection' (*op. cit.*) but a series of partial
alterations and compromises in the regulation of the balance towards social progress.

Because of this relationship between planning and democracy,
it will be inevitable that the social planner will be drawn into
the developing arena of 'public participation in planning'. One
cannot act on behalf of society without establishing patterns of

communication with people and groups in order to understand problems, and interpret requirements and aspirations. In this process of communication new ideas are being forged which will considerably affect both democratic institutions and the organization of planning. In this connection, in an effort to stimulate public participation the Town Planning Institute has quite properly recognized a twofold objective: that of 'making local planning authorities *better* local planning authorities and the public better able to recognize good planning and distinguish from bad, to demand the good from the local authorities representing it, and be readier to put public interest before private gain in so doing'.[2]

The planner is still very much at the threshold of developing participation techniques. There is a good deal of experiment to be done, and because some of the early attempts will concern detailed proposals for particular communities, the specialist social planner will have a valuable contribution to make. His 'feel' for community requirements will help in the developing dialogue between planner and planned.

American experience will be highly relevant. Three case studies by Davies of the role which neighbourhood groups have played in urban renewal in New York provide an example, dealing with the question of formation of neighbourhood attitudes, and the role of neighbourhood and non-neighbourhood actors in their attempts to exercise influence. Davies's observations will strike responsive chords in the minds of planners in this country who have dealt with representatives of local associations.

> Aside from the benefits to be gained and the probability of successfully exercising influence, the most important factor determining the degree of involvement of a neighbourhood group in a renewal controversy is the cohesiveness of the group. The group's cohesiveness on the renewal question will depend upon the relationship between the shared interests that provide the basis for the group and the stakes of the individual group members in the renewal controversy. The more closely related the basis of the group to the stakes of the members, the more uniform will be the attitude of the members towards the proposed project and the more cohesive the group will be.[3]

In dealing with neighbourhood groups at this level, planning takes on a new dimension because this aspect of social planning necessitates a new involvement in a political process. 'To give vitality to planning and reality to the plans that are produced, one must infuse the planning process with the realism brought by political engagement.'[4] In this process the social planner should have much to contribute.

These thoughts on public participation remind us that town planning has evolved with two distinct though complementary meanings. In its technical sense it might be considered as a process in the borderland between politics and management. But in its ideological sense planning is a means for achieving a measure of self-direction in the evolution of a social system. In the words of Friedmann, 'the utopian element in human thought has fastened on to planning as its particular vehicle and method of expression'.[5] This second interpretation of planning has been neglected and now needs re-emphasis in order to lead to a new evaluation of town planning itself and recognition of social planning as a complementary field.

The legislation of 1909 regarded the concern of planning primarily as the improvement of urban housing conditions. But there were also additional inherent overtones of the Garden City reformers who were not merely concerned with environmental improvement but who also set out to create satisfactory communities. The challenge for planning now is to interpret the fundamentals of the movement and the character of its evolution for present-day circumstances. Stripped to essentials, a basic goal has been and is now to ensure that physical plans serve social needs.

In the evolution of planning, the sequent interpretation and realization of objectives has to be seen against a backcloth of changing situations. In the first place there has been increasing public intervention in national housing, and social and economic affairs and a range of legislation has given wide powers to planning and other agencies. Secondly there are new environmental factors to consider; planning for better living conditions does not stop at housing but involves consideration of a range of issues concerning the environment. In this way twentieth-century planning has developed a body of knowledge with successive accretions of related interest and concern around a core philosophy.

In this evolution planning has tended to rely heavily on a physical role concerned with the allocation and use of land and the character and siting of buildings rather than seek the full harmony of physical development designed to meet social needs. There are substantial arguments against maintaining this narrow interpretation. On the one hand we cannot ignore the social aspects which have fashioned the origins of the planning movement, and on the other, experience clearly shows that planning does not stop at *plan making* but the process continues with *plan implementation* involving not only physical but also social and economic considerations. Moreover, the environment with which the planner is concerned should now be regarded not merely as a physical entity, but as one in which individuals and social organizations exist and to which the process of planning should be equally relevant. Social planning is therefore the third part of a town planning trilogy, inseparable from aspects of physical and economic planning within a total discipline.

Social planning defined in this way is broad and all-embracing. As suggested on page 1 the term may have a number of different meanings of varying relevance for the planner. There may even be international misunderstandings as to what is implied. In America for example social planning may be thought of in much the same light as a community project, but this would not be sufficient. In the United States there has been a flowering of community enterprises, initiated largely outside the framework of local government and undertaken by a proliferation of civic associations and citizen committees. There has been a host of projects for 'improvement'; in the field of urban renewal the Hyde Park–Kenwood project in Chicago is well known, but in the main the schemes have been relatively non-controversial, for example relating to educational or youth facilities. These projects have been supported by voluntary institutions ranging from the more permanent varieties such as the Community Chest, Chamber of Commerce and service clubs to the *ad hoc* Citizens Committees; in initiating change and marshalling public support they may, in many ways, be object lessons for similar British activity. But this is not social planning as the town planner sees it: his concept is much more integrative. Local community action as in the American situation may be most important and relevant, but I am anxious to present the planner's view of social planning on a quite different scale.

The wider interpretation of the context of town planning helps us to break away from past constraints, where a particular overt influence has been the canon of environmental determinism. We can in fact suggest the planner's role to be permissive as much as authoritarian. His task now may be thought of as to plan for social needs not in a direct way by shaping a physical environment and anticipating a particular kind of social response but largely in an indirect way by presenting opportunities and providing satisfaction, the argument being that needs are determined best by the exercise of choice amongst alternatives. The key therefore is to see planning's role to develop the potentialities of life by revealing to people what can be done and what is available. As a corollary, it becomes clear therefore that planning is not a social reform movement; it holds no lofty view as to the purposive functioning of society. It may indirectly achieve many of the aspirations of social reformers, but this is not planning's purpose.

These objectives, centred round opportunity and satisfaction, belong to town planning itself. Within the complementary field of social planning which we have defined, more specific objectives have been suggested. In the first place, we have indicated that the promotion of human contact should be sought in order to satisfy individual human needs and to develop a vitality within society. Secondly, there are the interests of minority groups to consider; these might include for example residents of disadvantaged areas, focussed on particular localities, or disadvantaged groups, such as the poor, who might be found anywhere. These groups will be unable to take full advantage of the universal provision of resources or facilities, and selective support will be required; in this support the social planner will have a contributory and co-ordinating role to play amongst a number of different agencies. Thirdly there is the contribution to the strengthening of social services; here the social planner might act as a central intelligence body. Fourthly there is the question of attempting to decide on priorities, the most difficult field of all.

Prior to this review of the scope and content of social planning, we looked briefly at the way in which community planning in the broad sense had been seen in the past and what particular contributions, especially in the nineteenth century, were influential in the history of planning. These antecedents suggest that the development of town planning during the present century has stemmed from two main roots. In the first place there has been concern for urban form and the search for the ideal city in architectural terms; and secondly there has been the search for the ideal community. Our concentration, by definition, has been on the latter. The long tradition of utopian thinking came to a head in the nineteenth century when profound urban and social changes both made possible and demanded new improvements. Following a lengthy period of agitation and practical experiment the emergence of a town planning movement may be considered part of that period of reform, of humanitarianism and democratization.

The origins of town planning in this country were therefore inspired particularly by social considerations, the fundamental questions first being the improvement of sanitary conditions and quality of urban life, and then housing. The turning point was when planning became firmly integrated with the housing reform movement and with attempts to control the distribution and manner of development of residential land. The creation of Model Towns and, later, Garden Cities gave to town planning its recognizable characteristic, and these experiments coloured the nature of the movement. During the twentieth century, the subsequent history of the movement has been disappointing: this is not to say that planning has not made great strides, but rather that progress has been accompanied by a departure from the social context of the activities which gave it birth. The concept of social planning, where it has been held at all, has been largely seen to operate in the creation of new settlements and has been thought of as dependent on new urban forms, a characteristic which reflects the traditional determinist outlook of the planner. The challenge and opportunities presented by communities in existing towns and situations has been neglected, an imbalance of focus which must now be redressed.

In defining a field of social planning, we reviewed the wide range of relevant factors which it might be thought to comprise. In the first place, we argued that if we are concerned with social and economic criteria, just as much as with the physical factors in the environment, then the planner should seek a far greater understanding of the complex interrelationships of environmental ecology. A feature of present-day town planning is that it puts its reliance on long-term physical objectives because of a primary concern with finite physical sciences. But with a greater concern for the social sciences, the importance of social and economic forces as dictates in environmental change is recognized, and increasing value seen in short-term objectives. This is not to deny the importance of long-term aims, but the implications suggest flexible goal setting, in full appreciation of social and economic issues.

We have suggested that we should recognize the city as a social system in action, as much as an artifact with a land use pattern. In other words we should regard the urban process as the evolution of a socio-cultural system as well as the evolution of a spatial settlement system. Social structure interacts with spatial form, and while the two are different, the town planner is concerned with both. This being so, an adaptive approach to planning will increasingly be required not necessarily to replace, but to be a more equal partner to a traditional static concept, and this will involve a radical challenge to accepted thinking and customary lines of approach to planning problems. In short, we should see society not as the end product of planning, as perhaps the determinist planner would view it, but as a starting point in planning. By tradition, town planning has seen the creation of a satisfactory physical environment as a medium whereby happiness in society might be achieved. The social planning view which we have put forward would not rely on such a causal relationship.

The social planner must clearly be cognizant of the many community studies which have been carried out in this country and elsewhere and by reading widely in other disciplines should be familiar with changing social conditions. For example there are the effects of long-term changes to consider in society, wrought by urbanization or industrialization and structural changes between classes. More specifically in the short-term there are social forces which are affecting changes in particular requirements, for example in housing, and these have to be evaluated much more carefully than a physically oriented planning process has been able to do so far. In addition, the social planner may make a contribution to a number of particular issues: we have suggested for example the factors affecting population movement, the question of the relationship between environment and behaviour, social changes in rural areas, and the wide field of leisure and recreation.

Recognition of these fields allows the planner to prepare a framework of social planning policies. We have suggested that at the heart of such guidelines must lie the clear difference between the concepts of social *engineering* and social *evolution*. Planning traditionally has seen its role in engineering terms, assisting in the fashioning of communities. This was made possible by a determinist philosophy and encouraged by a long history of practical experiments, not the least of which were the Model Towns and Garden Cities with which the very birth of planning was associated. As such, social planning was seen as a social reform movement championing the aim of desirable, balanced communities. In definitive terms this proved impossible, but planning has all too often continued to follow obsolete objectives.

But the keynote of social planning is social evolution: the

objectives of planning are to facilitate individual creativity within society and to remove constraints on social change and on particular groups sharing in the advantages of that change. Social planning opens the gate to opportunity whereby choice might be exercised. Social reformers within this context may encourage movements in one way or another, but that is a different question: the social planner is the midwife but not the parent of an ideal community.

From this starting point we have suggested that social planning strategy should be designed to limit those social, physical and economic constraints which operate in the environment as well as within the institutional framework in such a way as to preclude individuals from fully experiencing or sharing in the conditions for maximum human happiness. Such an approach influences the consideration of a host of policies throughout the whole of town planning, social, economic and physical.

For example it reinforces the view, as we have seen, that an adaptive approach to planning should be seen as of equal relevance to a static approach, depending on the circumstances. It is not necessarily the case that planning solutions should always be *optimum* solutions over the long-term; equally they might simply be *better* solutions over the short-term. A pertinent practical issue is of course in planning proposals for twilight areas where a number of social and economic criteria may effectively preclude the adoption of optimum standards.

Additionally there is a wider implication. By tradition, the extension of facilities throughout the community has been in the form of universal provision. But the needs of the community are not uniform and planning should increasingly recognize the need to identify underprivileged areas, both geographically and within the socio-cultural system, for enhanced attention. Just as some people, such as problem families or the poor or immigrants, fail to take advantage of benefit applied universally, so do some communities in particular areas whether they are rural, urban or more broadly of a regional nature.

In the context of these considerations we have shown how social planning policies might be framed in respect of national and regional matters, community planning at the neighbourhood level, housing matters and urban renewal. Additionally the social planner will be able to play a contributory and 'intelligence' role in respect of individual problem groups within society as well as in social administration generally. Finally, policies for leisure and recreation will be fashioned in the light of examination of changing social criteria.

The preparation of these policies will be facilitated by the recognition of a social plan to accompany the more traditional planning reports. Planners have become accustomed to the development plan of a local authority as a medium for diagnosing particular situations and outlining future policies. There has been heavy reliance on the physical aspects of planning in these documents and proposals have been itemized (for Ministry approval) in some detail. We might now postulate a social plan as a complementary document, although there will be important differences in presentation. This will be a declaration of policy which will rely on a framework of intent rather than a series of detailed proposals. Moreover this will be a report notable as a co-ordinator of many departments' work. It might be argued that the typical local authority physical plan is also a co-ordinator by virtue of its land allocation function, but in practice it is the financial programme which provides a more realistic short-term framework for departmental projects.

The social plan will analyse the relevant problems of the local authority in question. As a background there will be the sociological changes inherent in a dynamic society. Some of these aspects will relate to structural matters over the country as a whole or a particular region; others will be pertinent to the local authority. The structural changes relate to the massive shifts which are taking place in society, such as the extension of further education, realignment in class structure, changes in kinship networks, and changes in social values and aspirations as reflected for example in housing or recreational habits.

Then there will be the local situation to examine, and the social plan should reveal pertinent facts of location: in urban areas this will include such as the distribution of social malaise, the problem family and social problems of various kinds, loneliness, poverty, homelessness, and the immigrant. Case studies of problem neighbourhoods will provide a focus of attention on priority areas where extra investment of financial and human resources will be needed.

As a policy statement the social plan will first of all indicate those objectives which are to be met as part of ongoing physical development. For example, with regard to housing and neighbourhood design, planning for consumer satisfaction will have bearing on the provision of facilities for contact and the formation of informal groups (as in play areas or shopping) and in the provision and distribution of social facilities and services. Secondly there will be an indication of the intelligence role which the social planner might perform in respect of welfare agencies generally. Thirdly there will be an identification of social priority areas, and a review of the social needs of those communities and the way in which they might be better met on a co-ordinated basis.

All this can be done as a policy document for a particular town and city. Much the same sort of approach can be adopted for rural areas. Regional and national social plans will be complementary to physical and economic strategies where broad statements of analysis and intent are required.

In cities the social priority area is also likely to be an action area from the statutory planning point of view. Again, just as a detailed physical appraisal is required, so will a detailed indication of the social aspects be needed. The physical plan will highlight the environmental deficiencies of, let us say, a twilight area. The social planner will at the same time present his analysis of the related situation. The use of Census material will assist substantially in identifying the major socio-economic characteristics, but the collection of further profile data will be needed for an evaluation of local and personal factors in depth. A household questionnaire based on the theme 'who lives where, in what and why' might be the basis of further information. The aspects where these additional data are required will be demographic (profile data), accommodation and facilities, tenure and rent, satisfaction with accommodation and with environment, household health and use of social services, social contact and leisure activities, an inventory of relevant household possessions, social attitudes and future household intentions. Such a survey might be linked with the first publicity of an improvement scheme; questions might be asked about attitudes to improvement and these may stimulate the emergence of local residents' groups as an exercise in community participation. The principle here would be that the local residents are likely to be in a far better position than anyone else to know what their needs are and what are the desirable housing and environmental solutions.

While the physical planner is carrying out his house condition survey there might be a general survey of households and their accommodation, for example age structure and size of households, number of rooms occupied, number of bedrooms, multi-occupation, household amenities, and net weekly incomes.

Evidence of social problems might be collected from a range of sources such as the Regional Hospital Board, the Chief Constable, Probation Officers, Medical Officer of Health, Housing Manager, Social Case Workers, N.S.P.C.C., Council of Social Service, and immigrant bodies.

Additionally, evidence will be required of the nature of community life to supplement the suggestions made at the time of the household survey. A useful review can be given by contacts with local doctors, estate agents, solicitors, men's clubs, child welfare clinics, health visitors and social workers, family planning clinics, young people's associations, youth clubs, the Children's Officer, Probation Officer, Children's Holiday Scheme, adult education classes, tenants' associations, over-60's clubs, local councillors, churches, N.S.P.C.C., Council of Social Service, playgroups, Immigrant Associations, Marriage Guidance Council, Department of Health and Social Security, Housing Advisory Bureaux, Association for the Unmarried Mother and her Child, neighbourhood associations, and a host of voluntary agencies, such as those for the elderly.

It has been a theme of this book that the social aspects of such an action area will contribute markedly to the nature of the physical proposals for improvement. 'Sameness' of approach with heavy reliance on standards to which the area must be upgraded will be a process which the social planner usually finds too rigid; differences in local situations should be accommodated and reflected in policies for the future.

The social planner's role will continue in the implementation of the proposals. His intelligence role has already been mentioned and his involvement in projects of community participation will be inevitable. Thereafter, much will depend on administrative measures. Within a local authority for example there is the possibility in the future of strong social welfare departments; but additionally there is the need to secure effective co-ordination of a host of voluntary agencies and the churches. Organizations will be required at different levels: there is the central co-ordination for a given town or city, as well as area-based co-ordination where local committees are invaluable. Only by means of an improved administrative framework will the social plan be an effective instrument in securing the harmony of social and physical planning.

This review of the scope of social planning and the part played by the social plan is of immense relevance for town planning as a whole. Appreciation of the content of the subject matter and its philosophical grounding, the evaluation of pertinent issues within its area of concern and the framing of policy, helps not only in the very recognition of social planning but in the reassessment of town planning as a parent body. The identification of the separate fields of physical, economic or social planning can be for convenience only; the main emphasis must be the totality of the whole of the planning process. At the moment there is not only a lack of co-ordination between the disparate elements, but also a reluctance to achieve this comprehensive outlook. This is not an academic issue, but is of immediate practical relevance. For example there is the necessity to ensure that physical development goes hand in hand with social development; the relatively feeble achievements in this direction since the war are eloquent testimony of the need for different concepts and improved administrative processes.

We have already mentioned the reluctance of planners to take this total view of their discipline. Lichfield for example at the height of the Town Planning Institute membership debate in 1966 gave his views as follows: '. . . it is easy for us as planners to see the need for social and economic planning and to press for appropriate measures. But despite our contact with such issues, physical planners as such are not equipped to plan for them and should not, in my view, feel that they themselves are not doing their job unless they start planning directly for all human activity.'[6]

A year later Kantorowich, to whom had been given responsibility for drawing the Town Planning Institute's new examination policy, concluded:

. . . Town Planning . . . has emerged fully in response to a social need as a distinct professional process, interposed as a catalyst between the stages of policy-making and implementation in the process of environmental change. It is dedicated to the promotion of an efficient and life-enhancing relationship between man and his physical environment. Town planning is a process, involving a recurring cycle of operations, for preparing and controlling the implementation of plans for changing systems of land-use and settlement of varying scale, ranging from a small local area at the one end to a complex region or complete country at the other.[7]

These views have not gone unchallenged. Burns for example in his Presidential Address of 1967 to the Institute approached his theme with the question 'What does man want out of life?', suggesting that:

We are concerned with:

a. man's need for personal relationships;

b. his need for freedom of choice;

c. the means whereby he can enjoy the kind of life he chooses; and

d. the restrictions he has to accept in the interests of seeing that he does not unduly restrict the legitimate achievement of other men's aspirations.[8]

He went on to conclude:

. . . We now are approaching the stage where comprehensive social planning is unavoidable if we really believe in the love of human beings. We must hope that those who work in this field professionally will become better organized as a group, and we may then see the emergence of a wholly new breed of planner concerned with social planning. My plea is that the chartered town planner must be associated with this new development, must welcome it, and must ensure that planning and social planning go hand in hand with common objectives and constant interchange of views on problems and ideas.

The difference between these attitudes is very wide, and the implications for the Town Planning Institute and the role of the professional planner are serious. On the one hand the Institute may prefer to have a 'narrow' view of planning, largely interpreted in physical terms relating to land use, in which case the situation will continue whereby many who are engaged in what is in fact the planning process will be excluded from professional recognition, of whatever status. This will always encourage the emergence of specialist interest groups within planning but outside the profession, and consequently the likelihood of allegiances to bodies other than the Institute. On the other hand if planning were to adopt the 'wider' view then the question of membership and educational policy would be very much back in the crucible of debate.

The planning profession was set up relatively late in the history of professional bodies. A number of effective associations had been founded before the nineteenth century, the earliest being the barrister in the fifteenth century followed by physicians (1518), apothecaries (1617), solicitors (1739), surgeons (1745) and veterinary surgeons (1791). But the nineteenth century saw the creation of many more, such as the civil engineers (1818), architects

(1834), pharmacists (1841), chemists (also 1841), mechanical engineers (1847), actuaries (1848), accountants (1853), dentists (1855), surveyors (1868) and teachers (1870).[9] With this formidable flowering it is no small wonder that the Town Planning Institute has found it hard going to establish itself as a powerful body especially when Institutions with overlapping interests had such an early start.

It is likely that the Institute will continue to find difficulties; these will be of a particular kind while ever a narrow view of planning prevails. Not only will some of its own members find dissatisfaction in a restrictive (and in my view, erroneous) interpretation of planning's role, but the voice of the professional body will be muted on issues which are important. At the present time it must be doubted whether the Institute in its present form, from the point of view of its outlook, is adequate to represent planning as it should be conceived. It could in fact be argued that the present character of the Institute is actually a hindrance to, rather than a promoter of, effective comprehensive planning, because it fights shy of the philosophy which makes it possible.

Indeed it might be argued whether planning needs an Institute at all. It might be claimed that planning ideology is best expressed and developed in a non-professional forum with free interchange of ideas; or that planning is an attitude rather than a body of technical expertise, and therefore not suitable for professional context; or that existing professional bodies might reasonably share and be responsible for the technical content of the subject matter. But an Institute exists and it is clearly better to optimize its merits rather than despair over its shortcomings. The key question is whether the wider interpretation of planning, giving full reign to the social content, would result in a weaker professional situation.

The core of planning has been established; there is an intellectual basis with a central body of knowledge to which accretions of related fields of interest have been added. No other single professional body fulfils the total technical role—whether it be plan making, allocation of resources, or co-ordination of technical services in the management of environmental change. No other body relates that technical role to an ideological social base, however widely and differently that might be interpreted. The widening of the disciplinary base would therefore not weaken the professional body, but strengthen it (albeit necessitating change) by giving full expression to its total philosophy. The Institute cannot for much longer continue to promote the image of a body concerned with only part of planning; a substantial realignment of outlook is required.

In conclusion, we should stress that the purpose of this book has been to show how social planning might be defined as a subsidiary field within planning itself. The ease with which this field might be recognized is of course an indication of the nature of planning, because as we have suggested, the social origins of the movement are still clearly in evidence. The views expressed stem from a broad view of planning, not merely the broad view of a planner: physical, social and economic planning is a trilogy, and the component parts only make sense in a total context.

The social planner has been presented as a particular specialist contributing to planning just as the regional planner does, or the architect planner or the transportation planner. For many reasons his contribution as a specialist is being made later than others. To some extent this is because social planning did not have the tools of the job until fairly recently: in some ways it had to wait for sociology and the techniques of social analysis to catch up. This is rather different from, for example, the case of the transportation planner whose new expertise was as dependent on an entirely new situation (the motor-car) as on techniques (the computer).

The recognition of the social planner as a specialist poses the question as to whether he should best operate within or outside a planning team. The immediate practical relevance of this concerns local authority planning work, where the social planner, because of the importance of his co-ordinating role and his intelligence function *vis-à-vis* other departments and agencies, might be seen most favourably placed outside the Planning Department. This might be opposed on two counts. Firstly any member of a specialist group within a team naturally wishes to be in a position to influence 'at the top', and this can best be done within the one department. Secondly, social planning occupies much too great an integrative position within the total planning process for an administrative divorce to be countenanced; the fate of social planning for too long has been to be regarded as an afterthought rather than a prior consideration.

In presenting the role of the social planner it has only been possible to review the situation in the most general way. Almost every section of the book is capable of considerable expansion, but this must be the work of subsequent contributors. The aim has been to extract significances from the origins and contemporary nature of planning philosophy and practice. In so doing, the exercise is doubly salutary: it clarifies for us the spirit and purpose of planning, and defines a subsidiary field of interest with its own specialist area of concern.

REFERENCES TO CHAPTER 5

1. Leonardo Benevolo, *The Origins of Modern Town Planning* (trans.), Routledge & Kegan Paul, 1967.
2. 'Public Participation in Planning. Memorandum of evidence submitted by the Town Planning Institute to the Skeffington Committee',* *Journal of the Town Planning Institute*, Vol. 54, No. 7, July/August 1968.
3. J. Clarence Davies, *Neighbourhood Groups and Urban Renewal*, Columbia University Press, 1966.
4. J. Clarence Davies, *op. cit.*
5. John Friedmann, 'Planning as a Vocation', *Plan*, Vol. 6, No. 3, 1966.
6. N. Lichfield, 'Objectives for Planners', *Journal of the Town Planning Institute*, Vol. 52, No. 8, 1966.
7. R. H. Kantorowich, 'Education for Planning', *Journal of the Town Planning Institute*, Vol. 53, No. 5, 1967.
8. Wilfred Burns, 'Presidential Address', *Journal of the Town Planning Institute*, Vol. 53, No. 8, 1967.
9. Barrington Kaye, *The Development of the Architectural Profession in Britain*, Allen & Unwin, 1960.

* The Skeffington Committee published its report in July 1969, entitled *People and Planning: Report of the Committee on Public Participation in Planning*.

Index

Abrahart, Councillor B. W., 5
Akroyd, Colonel Edward, 29
Aldridge, Henry R., 43
Alexander, Christopher, 119–20
Andreae, Johann Valentin, 14–15
Anti-urban tradition, 117–18
Aquinas, St Thomas, 10
Ashton under Lyne, 17
Athens, 118
Auden, W. H., 48
Augustine, St, 10

Bacon, Francis, 14–15
Banbury, 63
Bellamy, Edward, 27, 32
Benevolo, Leonardo, 163
Berinsfield, 74–5
Berkshire, 105
Bethnal Green, 64
Betjeman, John, 144
Birmingham, 30–1
Birmingham, Bournville, 30–1, 43
Birmingham conurbation, 128
Birmingham, Harborne, 34
Birmingham, Ladywood, 83
Birmingham, Sparkbrook, 101, 149
Birmingham, University of, 7
Booth, Charles, 17
Booth, General William, 24
Bournville, 30–1, 43
Bracey, H. E., 75
Bradford, 29
Bristol, 20, 64, 75, 151
British Travel Association/University
    of Keele, 111

Broadacre City, 37
Bromborough Pool, 30
Brook Farm, 23–4
Buckingham, James Silk, 25–6, 32, 42
Burns, John, 34, 42
Burns, Dr Wilfred, 3, 174

Cabet, Etienne, 24
Cadbury (brothers), 30–1, 43
Calhoun, John, 85–6
Campanella, Tomaso, 14–15
Censuses of 1961 and 1966, 89, 93
Central Housing Advisory Commit-
    tee, 135
Central Housing Advisory Sub-Com-
    mittee, 152–3
Chartist Co-operative Land Com-
    pany, 23–4
Chaux, 21
Chicago, 90, 166
Christian, John, 85
Cité Industrielle, 37
Citizen (public) participation, 6, 164
Colchester, 157
Coleridge, Samuel Taylor, 19–20
Collison, Professor P., 5
Columbus, Ohio, 75
Community action, 166
Community experiments, 20–4
Community studies, 63–4
Crestwood Heights, 71
Crichton, Ruth, 105
Crossley, Sir Francis, 29
Crossley, John, 29
Crossley, Joseph, 29

Croydon, 96

Davies, J. Clarence, 164
Davies, J. G., 5
Donne, John, 50
Dower, Michael, 109
Doxiadis, Constantinos A., 118
Dwellings, size-distribution of, 138

Earswick, 30
Eliot, T. S., 49–50
Embourgeoisement, 73
European Coal and Steel Community, 49
Exeter, 91

Family, the, 69
Family Service Unit, 6, 147
Florence, 11
Foley, Donald L., 115–17
Forshaw, J. H., and Abercrombie, Patrick, 130
Fourier, Charles, 23, 37
France, Anatole, 117
Frankel, Charles, 69
Fried, Marc, 83
Friedmann, John, 165

Garden Cities and Town Planning Association, 43
Garden City, 31–3
Garden City Association, 33, 43
Garden city movement, 33, 37
Garnier, Tony, 36–7
Geddes, P., 16, 38
Glossop, 17, 63
Goldthorpe, John H., 73
Gosforth, 63
Greater London (see also London), 95–6, 106

Halifax, 29
Hall, Peter, 77
Hammersmith, 77
Hampstead Garden Suburb, 34, 43
Harborne (Birmingham) Garden Suburb, 34
Harrington, James, 14
Hertfordshire, 106
Hertzka, Theodore, 24
Hill, Octavia, 28–9, 58
Hobart, 90
Hobsbawm, E. J., 17
Hoggart, Richard, 71
Housing, 136–40
Housing associations, philanthropic, 29

Housing, Town Planning, etc., Act, 1909, 35, 42
Howard, Ebenezer, 24, 31–3, 43
Huddersfield, 17
Hull Garden Village, 30
Hunter, D. R., 48

Immigrant, coloured, 6, 101–3, 148–50
Industrial Revolution, 16–18
Industrialism, 68
Inner urban areas, 141–7

Jacobs, Jane, 61
Jennings, Hilda, 64, 141
Jesuits, 15
Johnson, Lyndon B., 101
Juvenile delinquency, 90–1, 93, 147

Kantorowich, R. H., 174
Keeble, Lewis, 45
Kirkup, James, 70
Kropotkin, P., 23–4
Krupp family, 30

Le Corbusier, 37
Ledoux, Claude Nicolas, 21
Lee, Terence, 134–5
Leicestershire, 74
Leisure and recreation, 7, 107–11, 155–60
Letchworth, 31, 33, 37, 43
Lethaby, W. R., 28
Lever, W. H., 43
Levittown, 72
Lewcock, Councillor Mrs C. M., 6
Lichfield, N., 174
Lightfoot Sports Centre, Newcastle, 158–9
Linear cities, 37
Liverpool, 64, 88, 90–1
Local communities, 74–6
London (see also Greater London), 88, 90, 95–6, 130
London, County of London Plan, 130
Loneliness, 96
Luton, 73

Manchester, City of Manchester Plan, 130
Marshall, Alfred, 32
Mason, Philip, 120, 149
Mata, Soria y, 37
Mead, Margaret, 118
Megalopolis, 118
Mental health, 95–6
Model communities (towns), 29–31
More, Sir Thomas, 10, 12–15, 49

Morelly, Abbé, 19
Morgan, John Minter, 23
Morris, R. N., and Mogey, John, 74
Morris, William, 26–8, 33
Mumford, Lewis, 10, 38
Musgrove, F., 82

National Committee for Common-wealth Immigrants, 101
National Housing Reform Council, 42
National Housing and Town Planning Council, 43
National Playing Fields Association, 157
Needs of New Communities, The, 152
Neighbourhood groups, 164
Neighbourhood planning, 129–36
Neighbourhood worker, 152
Newcastle upon Tyne, 88, 93, 97–8, 102, 138, 145, 147–8, 157–8
Newcastle, Bishop of, 5
Newcastle, *City Development Plan*, 3
Newcastle, City Planning Officer, 5–6
Newcastle, Director of Housing, 6, 98
Newcastle, Lightfoot Sports Centre, 158–9
Newcastle, Medical Officer of Health, 5–6
Newcastle, other Corporation Officers, 98
Newcastle, Jesmond, 6
Newcastle, Rye Hill, 4–6, 94, 145–6, 148
Newcastle, Scotswood Road, 4
New Lanark, 20
New Towns, 37, 132
Nicholas, R., 130
Nicholson, J. H., 152
Northern Region, 82, 124–7
North Kensington, 77
Nottingham, 100

O'Connor, Feargus, 23
Outdoor Recreation Resources Review Commission, 111
Overcrowding, 84–9, 93–4
Owen, Robert, 20–22
Owner-occupation, 139

Paddington, 77
Pahl, R. E., 106
Palmer, J. E., 111
Pantisocracy, 20
Participation—see Citizen (public) participation

Peabody, George, 29
Pemberton, Robert, 26
Penn, William, 15
PEP, 101
Phalanstère, 23–4
Philadelphia, 15
Philosophers, Ancient Greece, 11–12
Philp, A. F., 88, 99
Piedmont Industrial Crescent of North and South Carolina, 67
Planning Advisory Group, 6
Planning, static and adaptive, 59–61, 169
Plant, James, 86
Plato, 11, 49
Playgrounds, children's, 133
Plowden Report, 147
Population migration, 7
Port Sunlight, 30, 43
Poverty, 99–101
Power, Canon Norman, 83
Price's Patent Candle Company, 30
Problem families, 6, 88, 98–9, 147
Prophets, Old Testament, 10
Prostitution, 6, 148
Public (citizen) participation, 6, 164
Pullman, 30

Radiant City, 37
Recreation—see Leisure and recreation
Reeder, D. A., 77
Regional policies, 124–9
Rehabilitation (revitalization, improvement), 4, 141–6
Rehousing, 4
Reissman, Leonard, 68
Reith Committee on New Towns, 132
Rent, 139–40
Republic, 11
Residential migration, 81–3
Rex, John, and Moore, Robert, 149
Richardson, Benjamin Ward, 26
Roosevelt, Franklin D., 101
Rosser, C., and Harris, C., 69
Rossi, P. H., 82
Rural problems, 103
Ruskin, John, 27
Rye Hill, Newcastle, 4–6, 94, 145–6, 148

Sainsbury, Peter, 88
Salt, Sir Titus, 29–30
Saltaire, 29
Savonarola, Girolama, 11
Schuster Report, 44

Second homes, 105–6
Seebohm (Report), 154
Sheffield, 27, 134
Sheffield, Park Hill, 134
Sherrard, Thomas D., 54
Sitte, Camillo, 28
Sjaastad, Larry A., 81
Smith, Councillor T. Dan, 5
Social administration, 150–4
Social classes, 69–73
Social Development Officer, 152–3
Social engineering, 116, 169
Social evolution, 116, 169
Social malaise, 5, 88, 91, 94
Social Plan, 3, 171–3
Social problem areas, 72, 92
South Shields, 70–1
Southey, Robert, 19–20
Stengel, Erwin, 97
Suburban development, 35
Suicide, 88, 97
Sunderland, 138
Swansea, 64, 69
Swimming baths, 159

Tawney, R. H., 51
Telang, Sudha D., 6, 102
Theatres, 160

Thompson, Wilbur, 133
Titmuss, R. M., 88
Town Planning Institute, 45, 164, 174–6
Twilight areas (zones), 74, 76–80, 91, 143–6, 148, 152

Unwin, Raymond, 33
Urban park, 159
Urban renewal, 140–7
Urbanism, 65–8
Utopia, 12–15
Utopian heritage, 9–19

Vienna, 28

Wakefield, Edward Gibbon, 32
Waterlow, Sir Sydney, 29
Webber, Melvin M., 61
Wells, H. G., 117
Welwyn, 37
West Midlands, 127–9
Whitman, Walt, 118
Wickenden, Elizabeth, 54–5
Wilson, Roger, 55
Winterbottom, D. M., 157
Wirth, Louis, 66–8
Wordsworth, William, 19
Wright, Frank Lloyd, 37